To Dan Arnold

What a wonderful
time we had under
your leadership on
the Hosp. Bd. — thanks
for my time.

[signature]

HINES

A LEGACY OF QUALITY IN THE BUILT ENVIRONMENT

ESSAYS BY

MARK SEAL

WILLIAM MIDDLETON

LISA GRAY

HILARY LEWIS

LAURA ROWLEY

WILLIAM POORVU

DAVID CHILDS

RON NYREN

ROBERT A. M. STERN

WILLIAM MCDONOUGH

ANN HOLMES

JOE MASHBURN

FOREWORD BY

PAUL GOLDBERGER

FENWICK

Hines, USA Headquarters
2800 Post Oak Boulevard
Houston, Texas 77056-6118
www.hines.com

First edition
Printed in China

16 15 14 13 12 11 10 09 08 07 1 2 3 4 5

Library of Congress Cataloging-in-Publication Data

Hines : a legacy of quality in the built environment / essays by Mark Seal ... [et al.].
        p. cm.
    ISBN 0-9749510-4-8
    1. Hines, Gerald D. 2. Real estate developers--
United States--Biography. 3. Real estate development--
Environmental aspects--United States. 4. Land use--
Environmental aspects--United States. 5. Building--
Environmental aspects--United States. I. Seal, Mark, 1953-
    HD278.H557 2007
    333.33092--dc22
    [B]

                        2006034861

Fenwick Publishing Group, Inc.
3147 Point White Drive, Suite 100
Bainbridge Island, Washington 98110

Fenwick Publishing produces, publishes, and markets custom publications for corporations, nonprofit organizations, and individuals.

www.fenwickpublishing.com

President and Publisher: Timothy J. Connolly
Vice President, Development: Sarah Morgans
Designers: Kevin Berger and Kelly Pensell
Copy Editor: Betsy Holt
Proofreaders: Polly Koch and Laurie Gibson

Illustrations © Jennifer Mann

Fenwick Publishing extends grateful appreciation to George Lancaster, Jack Beuttell, and the corporate communications office at Hines for their efforts and insights during the production of this book.

All imagery is from the collections of Hines Interests Limited Partnership and its employees and alumni, and used by permission of Hines, except for pages 112, 114–115, 118, 121, 122, 124–125, 128, 133, 137, 138–139, 144, 150, 190, 192–193, 199, 203, 204–205, 223, 237, 238–239, 242–243, and 252, Keith Brofsky; 169, courtesy Robert A. M. Stern Architects; 176, courtesy Pei Cobb Freed & Partners; 179, courtesy Kohn Pedersen Fox Associates; 255, Ellsworth Kelly, *Color Panels for a Large Wall*, purchased with funds provided and promised by The Glenstone Foundation, Mitchell P. Rales, Founder © Board of Trustees, National Gallery of Art, Washington; 280-281, © Richard Page; 287, © Rice University; 284 and 289, courtesy the Yale School of Architecture; 291, Greg Betz; 292, Richard Leslie Schulman; and 294, Eddie Seal.

All photographs of archival prints, documents, and objects were taken by Fenwick Publishing.

CONTENTS

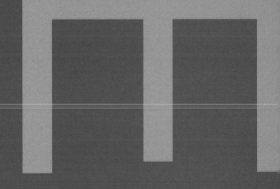

Foreword
by Paul Goldberger

"I am an American, and Paris is my hometown," the writer Gertrude Stein said, by which she meant she saw herself less as an expatriate than as someone who brought an American spirit abroad with her. Gerald Hines might go this one better and say that he is a Texan, and London is his hometown. Although Hines has lived primarily in London for more than a decade and his firm now works all across the world, his fundamental instincts are those of an American: he is open to new ideas; he has a passionate belief in the future; he believes deeply in democracy; and he has based his entire career as a developer on a certainty that design can, in some way, enhance the quality of life. ▣ I am not sure that any place other than Texas could have produced Gerald Hines, though it may be more accurate to say that he was also equally formed by his Midwestern beginnings, because what really characterizes Hines is a nearly perfect balance between realism and the capacity to dream. He is a pragmatist, and he is an optimist–at once matter-of-fact and daringly imaginative. Out of this combination has come one of the greatest careers in real estate of the last century. Gerald Hines is clearheaded. He is enthusiastic without being sentimental, and–perhaps most unusual of all for a real estate developer–he is almost unceasingly curious. He is interested in how people relate to buildings and how buildings shape cities and how technology changes the way people live and how aesthetic taste relates to the marketplace. He has brought to large-scale real estate development two things that, while not entirely unprecedented, were scarce indeed before he began doing the major projects for which he is known.

New York City's 53rd
At Third, nicknamed
the "Lipstick Building"
for its shape and
rosy hue, designed
by Philip Johnson
and John Burgee.
With this building,
says Paul Goldberger,
architecture critic
for *The New Yorker*,
Gerald Hines proved
that he could commit
to serious aesthetic
inquiry while producing
commercially viable
buildings.

The first is the structure of his firm, originally called Gerald D. Hines Interests and now, Hines. In the manner of a major corporation, Gerry Hines trained a whole cadre of executives and created a culture that more resembled that of the Fortune 500 corporations he wanted to attract as tenants than the typical real estate enterprise. The organizational culture of Hines is Gerald Hines' first major accomplishment, and it will extend long beyond his time.

Hines' second achievement has had a broader impact still. Before Hines built the Galleria, One Shell Plaza, and Pennzoil Place, his first major projects in Houston, real estate developers tended to shy away from architects with ambitious design intentions. Architects represented time, trouble, and expense—not added value, or so most developers believed. The rare office buildings designed by well-known architects were almost invariably corporate headquarters that companies built for themselves, not commercial structures a developer put up for profit.

Hines realized that if a company that was constructing a building for its own use could justify architectural distinction as a means of enhancing its identity—both as a form of advertising and also as a contribution to its employees and to the broader community—corporate tenants could be induced to see things the same way. A memorable design by a prominent architect might cost a little more, but it could also be vastly more profitable, both for Hines' tenants and for his company. And if the building became a local landmark, it would buttress Hines' own reputation as much as that of his tenants.

And so Hines went to Gyo Obata, Bruce Graham, Philip Johnson, I. M. Pei, Kevin Roche, and Robert A. M. Stern—to name just the first architects he worked with—and convinced them to produce commercial buildings that could satisfy a developer's economic demands while still meeting an architectural critic's expectations. Not every project became the landmark Hines wanted it to, but nearly everything the company built after Obata's Galleria in 1970 was notable for its ambition and, more often than not, distinguished in its results. Pennzoil Place, completed in 1975, marked both a turning point in the notable career of Philip Johnson, who before Hines' invitation to design the building had done almost no work for commercial developers, and a significant moment in the evolution of downtown Houston. With its dual towers separated by glass-covered lobbies, Pennzoil Place was one of the first skyscrapers in the 1970s to be noteworthy both as a pure essay in architectural form and as a major piece of public space. It was not the tallest building in Houston, but it was the one that exerted the most powerful magnetic force: Pennzoil was the first new office building that people went to downtown Houston specifically to see.

The relationship between Johnson and Hines was an extraordinary one—the cultivated Eastern aesthete and the daring Texas developer, each contributing something the other needed to make him whole. They learned from each other over the course of projects such as Post Oak Central, the Transco Tower (now Williams Tower), and the RepublicBank Center (now Bank of America Center) in Houston; 580 California in San Francisco; and 53rd At Third (the "Lipstick Building") in New York. Hines was determined to prove that being a patron and being a businessman did not have to be mutually exclusive, while Johnson wanted to show that his commitment to serious aesthetic inquiry and his desire to produce commercially viable buildings did not have to be mutually exclusive, either. If that relationship was particularly close—Hines, more than any other client, turned Johnson and his then-partner John Burgee from architects of small institutional buildings to shapers of the skyline—the remarkable meeting of minds that it represented was replicated to a certain extent in Hines' relationship with David Childs of Skidmore, Owings & Merrill; Cesar Pelli; Norman Foster; Stern; Roche; and numerous other architects. And where Hines went, so followed the real estate industry. By the 1980s, developers all over the country were viewing architecture as added value, and the marketplace had come to demand a different level of design seriousness. A cultural shift had occurred.

For me, architecture will be Gerald Hines' greatest legacy, since few people have done as much as he has to make architecture a truly public, and genuinely popular, art in our time. If architecture is a central part of the cultural dialogue today, Gerald Hines has done much to make it so, not by creating the most avant-garde pieces of architecture, but by commissioning the buildings that convinced the average person that architecture could be an exhilarating presence in the cityscape. Hines' story involves more than architectural patronage, of course. In the pages that follow, an array of essayists approach the subject of Gerald Hines and the company he founded half a century ago from a variety of vantage points. Business journalists, architects, academicians, critics, and feature writers make up the twelve contributors who offer varied and insightful perspectives on Hines, on the company's history, and on the legacy that Hines has established in the arts, education, and the environment.

Every one of these essays offers insight into Gerald Hines as a human being—each shows us some element of his extraordinary sensibility, and demonstrates Hines' ability to prove that the notion of a pragmatic visionary is not a contradiction in terms. And yet, for all the tribute these authors pay to Gerald Hines the man, every one of these essays also reminds us of something that Hines himself has always understood: if you are in the business of real estate, it is the buildings that matter. You are what you build, as Gerald Hines has demonstrated now for half a century.

Paul Goldberger
February 2007

SHINE LINES

THE MAN
THE HISTORY
THE APPROACH
THE LEGACY

1

A PROFILE

The 1943 yearbook
graduation portrait
of Gerald D. Hines at
Emerson High School
in Gary, Indiana. Hines'
earliest lessons in
conservative fiscal
management, which he
would later adopt in his
business, were learned
peddling newspapers
during the Depression.

NNAN

FREDERICK HASLETT

THOMAS

SON

GERALD HINES

SUE HOLN

From the heartland to the heart of world business: the Indiana native has lived in London since the mid-1990s. Hines launched operations in Europe after the fall of the Berlin Wall, spreading his formula for buildings that are both architecturally superior and commercially successful.

Gerald D. Hines: A Profile
by Mark Seal

We are halfway to the Milan airport when Gerald D. Hines reaches into his suit jacket pocket and pulls out the instrument that has guided his amazing fifty-year rise as the world's foremost commercial real estate developer. "Well, there it is," he says with the low-key enthusiasm that is his hallmark, producing a one-by-four-inch plastic slide rule and proceeding to show me how it works, multiplying, dividing, conjuring up square roots in seconds–precise data for a man of hard numbers and empirical facts. "Interesting, interesting," he says, returning the slide rule to his pocket as he settles in to focus on the summits to which this seemingly simple instrument has taken him. ◫ Through every phase of his career, Hines has depended on the slide rule to get answers fast. "Not a computer! A slide rule!" marvels his friend and early partner Houston developer Jerry Finger, who first met Hines in 1959. "When we were talking about doing a deal, he would move around on the slide rule and quickly compute the return on equity, the cost to build, the time value of money, which would take most people some time. He never generalized; he was always very precise in everything he did." ◫ It is 6:30 on a weekday morning in spring 2006 when we meet to discuss his life and career, and Gerald Hines is going to work in the world. After his customary steamed broccoli for breakfast, he has emerged from the Four Seasons Hotel in Milan, where his firm is developing a massive new city within the heart of the city, to head home to London. Now, with his jet grounded for service, he is flying Air France.

He seems not to mind one whit about joining the masses on a commercial flight, or that a writer, now beside him in the backseat of a car speeding to Milan's Linate Airport, would spend every minute of the journey pressing him for answers about his phenomenal career.

While the myth of Gerald Douglas Hines stands in steel and concrete in cities around the world, the man is more elusive. He downplays his brilliance, tenacity, and vision, stressing that his career was a slow and steady evolution, instead of one burst of genius after another. And when pressed to elaborate on why he did this or was drawn to that, he employs his favorite phrase of reflection: "Well," he says. "That was interesting."

"My husband? Oh, he's a builder," says Barbara Hines in summing up what drives Gerald. "Wherever he goes, anywhere in the world, he makes things happen, buildings sprout up. He loves beauty. He loves architecture. He loves to create really fine buildings that people feel proud of owning or being a part of. That's what drives him."

I look over at Hines in the backseat beside me, a calm, collected, almost serene gentleman of eighty, his laid-back exterior in stark counterpoint to his legendary fierce competitiveness and steely resolve. "Underneath, there is a quiet, constant tension, but he does not let it show," says his wife. But when you get down to the man, that is what you find.

■ ■ ■ ■ ■

"I discovered the slide rule under Mrs. Talbot," he says with a boyish grin. Mrs. Talbot was his math teacher at Emerson High School in his hometown of Gary, Indiana, the steel town named for Elbert H. Gary, the chairman of the U.S. Steel Corporation, which founded the town and whose mill there was once the world's largest. The Hines family came to Gary from an ancestry of the sea. "I lost two great-grandfathers, who were captains of fishing fleets, at sea," says Hines of his Nova Scotia sailing lineage. "One of them had a small farm and built all these little community churches throughout Nova Scotia. So I guess I've got building and seawater in my veins."

But his father, Robert Gordon Hines, was a steelworker. When jobs became scarce in Canada, they moved to Gary, then the world's biggest steel town. With their two kids, Gerald and Audrey, the Hineses were pretty much the typical Gary steelworker family. "He always knew what he wanted and he'd go after it," says his sister Audrey Hines Watt. "He was very determined. If he wanted to do something, he'd do it and he'd see it through."

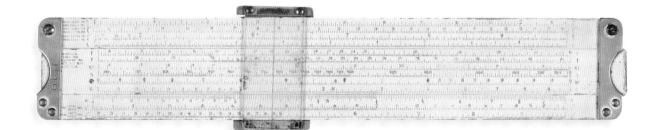

Hines' family roots include "building and seawater," as he puts it; his Canadian ancestors built community churches throughout Nova Scotia and ran fishing fleets. Hines says he owes some of his success to a high school math teacher who introduced him to the plastic slide rule. Hines could quickly compute the return on equity, the cost to build, and the time value of money of a specific development on his slide rule. Opposite, his personal slide rule has his initials carved into one side. Above left, Hines (second from left in the front row) with his high school cross-country team. Above right, Hines in 1944 as a second lieutenant in the U.S. Army Corps of Engineers. Hines was stationed in Fort Lewis, south of Tacoma, Washington.

THIS MEDAL IS
AWARDED TO
GERALD D. HINES
△△ '45
FOR HIS ACHIEVEMENTS
WHICH HAVE BROUGHT HONOR
AND PRESTIGE TO THE NAME
OF THE SIGMA CHI
FRATERNITY

Hines hadn't technically completed high school when he was accepted to Purdue University at age sixteen. He became a cheerleader at Big Ten basketball and football games, opposite, pledged Sigma Chi fraternity, and worked in the cafeteria to make ends meet. Hines studied engineering in part because his father advised him, "Engineers didn't get laid off during the Depression."

Young Gerry Hines had a paper route, lettered on his high school cross-country track team, and spent his free time building model airplanes. "Maybe that is the first aspect of building that I got involved in," he says. But until his high school teacher showed him the instrument of his destiny, Gerald Hines was uncertain about his future, knowing only–after a summer job in the steel mill–what he didn't want to do. "There's no way I wanted to work in a steel mill," Hines says. "I sold vacuum cleaners door-to-door, newspapers, shoes at Sears Roebuck. . . . " Then he found the slide rule, and the door to his future opened wide.

"It's just like a computer," he says, and as he works the slide rule, it becomes clear that it's much more than a mere calculator. "I could use the slide rule and come up with a multitude of answers. It also allowed me to think. So that was kind of an interesting ploy. When I wasn't sure I wanted to answer a question, I'd hit the slide rule and it would give me time to think."

There was only one career for a kid in love with the slide rule: engineering. "My father said, 'Engineers didn't get laid off during the Depression,' and the Depression was a major factor in the formation of my thoughts and background because it had such an impact on all of us." Or as he once told *Real Estate/Portfolio* magazine, "If you peddled papers in Gary, Indiana, during the Depression, you tend to think that someday the Depression will come back."

When it came time for college, Hines chose Purdue, a land-grant college blessed by the Morrill Act, whose mission was to provide members of the working class with a college education at a minimum cost. "That was a wonderful piece of education," he says. "It's the American dream."

Gerald Hines was standing on its precipice. "Purdue had an outstanding engineering school," he continues. "They flunked out two-thirds of the freshman class." Although he hadn't technically finished high school when he was accepted to Purdue at sixteen, he passed his freshman year. "To make ends meet, I worked in the cafeteria," he says. "Then, during that first year, I pledged Sigma Chi. We had a very interesting group of young men at the fraternity. That was an important part of my life, my growth, and just learning about people. Those were very formative years for me."

He spent his spare time in a role that would serve him well when it came time to champion development projects. "I got involved in cheerleading," he says. "When the head cheerleader left, I took over as head cheerleader for that semester. Well, it was interesting. It was fun in the Big Ten. We went to all the basketball games and football games, four boys and four girls. I did that until I left for the service."

He left college for a stateside stint as a lieutenant in the U.S. Army between 1943 and 1946. Then, after his graduation from Purdue in 1948, Hines went to work.

"I was hired by American Blower Corporation, manufacturers of technical equipment such as large fans for major buildings," he says. "After I finished the training course in Detroit, they gave me a choice of going to Indianapolis, Baltimore, or Houston, Texas."

■ ■ ■ ■ ■

The day before, at the headquarters of Hines Italy, I'd watched the master builder in his element: a brightly lighted room filled with multinational men and women, reviewing the elaborate design boards of eighteen major architects making proposals to design various buildings in Hines' new "city" in the middle of Milan. Among the young men on his own team, as well as visiting architectural masters and local government city planners, Hines acted as counselor, cheerleader, peacemaker, and, in the end, decision maker—although he always made the decisions a group effort.

"How do you get the most value?" he asked the group.

"We have to have something that the Milanese will be proud of, and the value will go up," he said.

And, finally, when he saw good, solid design that would last through the ages, he was ready to roll, full steam ahead. "These guys have mass appeal!" he exclaimed of one architect's proposal. "Bring 'em in, and let's get to work!"

After graduation from Purdue in 1948, Hines took a job with the American Blower Corporation, which made equipment for major buildings. Two years later, he became a sales representative for Claridge Fans and Kewanee Blowers, an experience that helped him learn about buildings inside and out. Hines in 1953, left, and with son Jeffrey Hines in 1956, when Jeff was one year old, below.

In that office, people hung on Gerald Hines' every word, a line of men and women awaited meetings, and his hours were scheduled minute by minute. But today in line to board the plane to London, he is anonymous, and I can imagine him when he moved to Houston: seemingly just another bachelor arriving in a capital of capitalism to stake his future. It was the fall of 1948, and Houston was the epitome of a boomtown. "Glen McCarthy [the model for Jett Rink in Edna Ferber's *Giant*] was opening the Shamrock Hotel, and, wow, what a party he threw!" Hines tells me. But the future developer of modern Houston, the man who would soon supercharge the skyline, arrived knowing no one except three fraternity brothers from Purdue. He checked into the YMCA, where, he says, he lived for two weeks before moving with his three friends into an apartment at 4011 Childress Avenue.

As always, Gerald Hines' goals were both simple and great. "I just wanted to succeed in Houston," he says.

After two years of crawling through basements and ductwork for American Blower Corporation, Hines discovered that working for a big corporation wasn't for him. He accepted an offer to become a junior partner in Texas Engineering Co., in the capacity of sales representative for Claridge Fans and Kewanee Blowers. Selling these products to mechanical contractors, Gerald Hines got to know buildings, both inside and out.

One Saturday night, in his apartment complex, the young sales rep, on a mission to gather guests for a party, began knocking on his neighbors' doors. One of them belonged to Dorothy Schwarz, a young woman working at what she thought would be a one-year job as an occupational therapist. "The first Saturday night I was there, I was in a baggy sweater typing a letter home and the doorbell rang and it was Gerry, inviting us to go to the party," Dorothy remembers.

She accepted the invitation. A few dates followed. "I think he said, 'Well, why don't you assume that every Saturday night you'll go out with me?'" Dorothy recalls. "He was somebody you really could trust. I admired his upbeat attitude toward everything. He was somebody I felt had a good sense of ethics, somebody I felt comfortable with."

After two years of dating, they went to visit Dorothy's parents at 1111 Park Avenue in Manhattan, the privileged address where Dorothy Schwarz, the granddaughter of the founder of the F.A.O. Schwarz toy store giant, had grown up. On March 8, 1952, they had a big wedding in New York City, then returned to Houston, where most expected Gerald Hines would continue his work as a sales rep, selling fans and blowers for office buildings. "Certainly, I had no idea about the tiger in his tank," Dorothy Hines says, "but he had a lot of energy. He was optimistic and always looked at the glass as half full."

They lived in a modest house in a modest suburb called Bellaire. One afternoon in their first year of marriage, in the boomtown that was soon to become insatiable for space, Gerald Hines found his future across his backyard fence.

Hines and his neighbor, Glen Dorflinger, were talking one evening when Dorflinger mentioned that the company for which he worked, the Fischer & Porter Company, needed bigger quarters, including a warehouse and more office space.

"Gerry said, 'Glen, let's build a building,'" Dorflinger remembers. "And I said, 'Gerry, what are you talking about? I don't have any money to build a building!' And he said, 'I don't have any money, either, but it won't cost much.'"

Gerald Hines knew buildings, but he also knew finance and, through his work in Texas Engineering, he knew how to keep a project's costs within control. "If you know math and you're an engineer, it's very easy to learn finance," says Hines. And the boomtown was ready to embrace the entrepreneur.

"There was a time in Houston where if you were building a house or a building you could borrow 100 percent of the property's value," says Dorflinger. "But you had to have a tenant before you could go to the bank and borrow the money."

Dorflinger called the president of Fischer & Porter and was told to submit a proposal. "Gerry said, 'There's some land on Richmond Avenue, and I have a friend who's an architect and he'll do the plans for two hundred dollars,'" Dorflinger remembers. The proposal was accepted, and Fischer & Porter became Gerald Hines' first tenant.

Hines took the signed lease to the bank and borrowed 100 percent of the construction cost—about $100,000—to go to work on his first building, 3,000 square feet of office space with a 2,000-square-foot warehouse at 3783 Richmond Avenue. Dorflinger reflects, "After about a year, Gerry said, 'Glen, let's build another building.' I said, 'Gerry, I don't think this is a good business. We've been doing it for a year, and we haven't made any money. You do it without me. You'll do all right by yourself.'"

■ ■ ■ ■ ■

Once again, Hines found himself at the right place at the right time. With no zoning restrictions, Houston was and remains arguably the most entrepreneurial real estate city in the world. "In Houston, you could start a building in sixty days," says Jerry Finger. "Today, it may take three months. But in LA, Boston, or New York

it takes three years. In no other city in the world could Gerry Hines take off as fast as he did in Houston."

But in that overheated, anything-goes market, which, Finger says, "attracted infinite gladiators and developers," Gerald Hines was an anomaly. First, he was an investment builder, "who builds and holds, instead of builds and sells," says Finger. Second, he never took the whole deal himself, but always enlisted investors. He began not with a grand plan, but a small niche and realistic expectations. "I did that on the side while I still had my engineering partnership, and I built about seven buildings that way," Hines says. "Then, after I had enough to create the cash flow, I resigned my position and recruited someone else to take my place. I went on to open an office at 4219 Richmond Avenue, which was the old GE Building. I started with a secretary, and that was it."

The secretary, Marian Dugdale, was still working at Hines as the company approached its fiftieth anniversary in 2007. "He had an office and I had the outside office, and I was Girl Friday," Dugdale remembers. "I collected the rent, paid the bills. . . . One time a lady came into our office and said, 'The water is leaking in the ladies room.' I said, 'Oh, I'm glad you told me. Mr. Hines will be right back.' She came back five minutes later and said, 'The water is now an inch deep.' Mr. Hines came back, rolled up his pant legs, and gave me a pail. He got a mop and started mopping the floor while I held the pail. Finally, he said, 'Marian, where's the water shutoff?' And I said I didn't know. He said, 'I'll go find it.' He cut off the water. The leak stopped and he said, 'Let this be a lesson. Whenever there's a water leak, don't mop the floor. Shut off the water first.'"

Although he built on other streets, he focused early on Richmond Avenue, a then sleepy road of small stores and old houses. By his second project, a 40,000-square-foot office/warehouse, he was already searching for ways to stand out from the pack. Hiring the former dean of the University of Texas architecture school, Walter Rolfe, Hines learned how architecture compounds a building's potential for success. "Rolfe showed him how to position a building to reflect light in a uniform way, how to use heavy doors and sturdy fixtures to give it character and substance," a writer for *Aspen* magazine reported in 1995. "Hines relished the process. He and Rolfe were able to build a better office warehouse than had ever been built in Houston. It attracted so much attention that Hines quickly got three other projects."

Hines recalls, "I suddenly realized that we'd hit upon a great marketing idea: good design at a reasonable cost. That's the system that evolved into the trademark of our company."

The new Hines trademark wouldn't be put into full effect on Richmond Avenue, but across a then-barren landmass a mile or so to the west—an area that would soon be intersected by the massive IH 610 freeway, which would ferry millions of motorists into the nexus of the new Houston and usher in a new era of American merchandising. The Galleria was a breakthrough multiuse development and shopping megalopolis befitting a boomtown.

■ ■ ■ ■ ■

Gerald Hines leans back in his airplane seat. "Well, that was interesting," he says of his start as a builder. But that was only the beginning. By the 1960s, Gerald and Dorothy were living on Radney Road in a midcentury modern house on three acres of wooded property in one of the villages west of Houston. They had two children, Jeffrey and Jennifer. Then, in 1963, Dorothy Hines got a call from her sister, who was working in the U.S. Department of State in Hong Kong. She had a cook, Mrs. Chen, whose son wanted to immigrate to the U.S. "It'll never happen, he's so far down the list, but if by some chance he clears the list would you take him in?" her sister asked. Dorothy consulted with Gerry, and they said yes. Sure enough, the list cleared, and not one Chen arrived, but the entire six-member Chen family. "He was the cook, she did the beds, and they became our family, the four children," says Dorothy Hines. "We put the kids through college. One went to Stanford and the oldest, Leo, works at Hines today as a senior vice president and fund manager of Hines' Emerging Markets Real Estate Funds."

"The Chen kids were just like brothers and sisters to Jenny and me," adds Jeff Hines.

On a weekend off in the early 1960s, Gerald and Dorothy took a vacation at a resort in Point Clear, Alabama. At the resort, they met Jane and Bruce Graham. Bruce was lead architect at Skidmore, Owings & Merrill, the venerable architectural firm responsible for Chicago's John Hancock Building and San Francisco's Bank of America World Headquarters. He would go on to design the tallest building in America, the Sears Tower in Chicago. After a weekend of golf, the two men decided it would be fun to do a project together someday.

In 1966, a new opportunity appeared: Shell, the oil giant, was seeking a developer to build its regional office in downtown Houston. Hines was a seemingly unlikely candidate: he had built only one high-rise, a sixteen-story apartment complex called The Willowick, in 1963. He'd just lost a contract to build the Houston Natural Gas Building, for which he'd used a local architectural firm. He wouldn't take that chance on Shell. "I said, 'I'm going to get a really outstanding architect this time, and I'm going to do an outstanding piece of architecture,'" Hines remembers.

Shell was so impressed with Hines' quality of work that it decided during construction to relocate its national headquarters from New York City to One Shell Plaza. Shell headquarters took over the building designated for regional, and the regional group ended up on the site that had been slated for offices above the garage—Two Shell Plaza.

"You have to be a pretty good promoter to talk Shell into hiring you to build a fifty-story building when the only other high rise you've done is an apartment complex," adds Jeff Hines, now president of Hines. "He's very understated, but he's one of the best presenters I've ever seen. The amount of enthusiasm he can put forth in a very genuine way is just very, very convincing. Because when he does something, he's a true believer, and that comes through. Dad has always had a passion for creating a great real estate project. He doesn't just view it as a financial play. He would get very involved in the details of whatever building he was building, down to what kind of hardware he was using on the doors of the warehouse. That attention to detail has permeated the firm, and it starts with a basic love of what he's doing."

Hines met Dorothy Schwarz in his Houston apartment complex in 1950, and they were married two years later. By the 1960s, Gerald and Dorothy were living on Radney Road in a midcentury modern house on three acres of wooded property in a village west of Houston. They had two children, Jennifer and Jeffrey.

For Shell, Hines immediately thought of Bruce Graham. "He and I went to see the chairman of Shell, and there were other architects making proposals," Graham remembers. "Gerry presented me . . . and said that I had done tall buildings before and so on. They asked me what the building would look like." Having no models of past skyscrapers to show, Hines focused on what he knew from experience: attention to detail. "He opened his briefcase and took out a sample of the solid-core door with its Siesziken German hardware and handle," says Graham. "He said, 'It would be like this.' Boom! He was saying that we were going to build a building as precise as this piece of hardware."

They won the commission. "Then, we went to build it, and of course it was a huge task. We were building the Galleria and Shell at the same time," says Gerald Hines.

The Galleria, a 600,000-square-foot mall announced in 1967, would set the new standard in malls across America. Hines found twelve acres on the southwestern border of the city at Westheimer and South Post Oak Boulevard, where Sakowitz and Joske's had built large stores. As always, he didn't do the deal alone. He assembled a group of investors to purchase the land, where he envisioned building a large shopping mall with a bank and a hotel on the premises. But what would the center be? Hines wasn't sure. With interest compounding, his investors were impatient to get the mall rolling. "None of us had the money to buy the land; I borrowed the money and was paying interest while

Gerry was fiddling with his slide rule, trying to come up with a concept," says John Duncan, former president of the Gulf+Western Company.

Once again, Hines turned to a great architect: the St. Louis–based firm of Hellmuth, Obata & Kassabaum. "Gyo [Obata] did some sketches, and we came up with the ice skating rink" as the center point of the mall, with all shops facing it. "He said, 'You ought to name it the Galleria," Hines remembers. "So I went and I saw the original Galleria." As always, he didn't want some here-today-gone-tomorrow building; he wanted something that would stand the test of time. Just as he would later do when developing the Aspen Highlands ski resort, for which he visited ten European ski mountains in five days by van, Hines flew to Milan to visit the Galleria Vittorio Emanuele II, which was built circa 1864. Standing in the soaring ancient glass-topped vault that became the world's first enclosed shopping mall, Hines could see the future: America's first true mixed-use center, a three-level, skylighted wonder designed and built to last.

As he had on his first building, Hines needed a tenant. Neiman Marcus, the legendary Dallas-based retailer, was considering building in Houston at another location. Hines found a way to bring them to the Galleria. "No rent," he told a group of Neiman Marcus family members and executives, including Stanley Marcus—meaning they could have the land in perpetuity in exchange for building a Houston Neiman Marcus and becoming the lead tenant in the Galleria.

Hines and architect Gyo Obata called a meeting of his investors in the Galleria at Houston's River Oaks Country Club. "I wasn't surprised; I was shocked!" remembers Duncan. "All of us who were minor investors were rather regional people. We expected a big, conventional mall, windows out front, parking in the back—and then we received Gerry's pitch. Number one, he had given the corner to Neiman Marcus. We were surprised to hear that the parking would be out front, and I remember thinking, 'Oh, God! No windows!' We were surprised to hear that there would be an ice rink, and all of the stores would face the ice rink—when there was no ice-skating in Houston. We were surprised to hear that there would be ten air-conditioned tennis courts on the roof. There were no air-conditioned tennis courts that we knew of."

It looked great on paper—but personally guaranteeing the construction costs of both the Galleria and Shell, which was $40 million alone, meant that the outwardly calm and collected Gerald Hines was up to his neck in risk. "The craziest thing in the world was to build those two big projects with the limited net worth that I had," he says. Particularly at a time when his net worth was $6 million in real estate. "Not much money in the bank. It was crazy, crazy, wild. Didn't sleep much. I'd get up at three or four in the morning."

With two mammoth projects, each with costs spiraling, Gerald Hines was about to become a cliché: the overextended developer whose dreams, and real estate, are seized by the bank. "I could have gone broke," Hines declares.

Instead, he went to the Houston-based Duncan brothers, for whom he had completed several building projects. John Duncan had founded the Gulf+Western Company, which went from automotive parts and financial services to publishing and entertainment (owning Paramount Pictures), and Charles Duncan had sold his Duncan Coffee Company to Coca-Cola. "Gerry does not act like a big-time real estate promoter," says John Duncan. "Nor is he a pound-the-table salesman. Quite the contrary. He acts like, I'm really a nice guy and I'm going to build you a great building, and you can just look me in the eye and tell how honest I am. And it works."

When Hines pitched Shell Oil to develop its regional headquarters in downtown Houston, his only previous experience building high-rises was a sixteen-story apartment building called the Willowick, left.

Gerald Hines with Houston mortgage banker Ben C. McGuire (left) and Hamilton Coolidge, vice president of New England Mutual Life Insurance Company, (center) at the signing of the permanent financing of One Shell Plaza. McGuire arranged the $35 million mortgage,which was the largest loan that New England Mutual had financed at the time.

"I went to John and Charles and I said, 'I know I'm going to need liquidity in these two projects, and you're a partner in the Galleria already. I'll give you a 5 percent interest in Shell and a 5 percent additional interest in the Galleria if you will loan me six million of your stock as collateral. I'll pledge all of my real estate to you, which is not liquid. But it will be liquid over time.'"

The Duncans agreed to loan him their stock as collateral, and the banks gave Hines some breathing room. "That was a crucial point in my evolution as a builder," Hines says.

He learned a lesson: Debt is Death. He would become known from then on for equity financing, instead of the conventional developer's habit of putting up a down payment and financing the rest. That approach would serve Hines well. When Congress repealed tax breaks on commercial real estate in the 1980s, most developers were forced to restructure. Some went broke. Hines was able to purchase $350 million of prime properties in default. In fact, Gerald Hines had such a reputation for financial integrity that in the late 1970s famed economist and then–Federal Reserve System chairman Paul Volcker asked Hines to chair the eleventh

district of the Fed under President Carter. "We had huge inflation: the interest rate on government bonds was 14 percent and 20 percent on loans," Hines remembers. "I learned a lot about inflation, I learned a lot about banking and, being chairman of the Dallas Fed, we had some very interesting times when the Hunts tried to corner the silver market."

For all of this, though, Hines displays no hint of accomplishment. His battle is against inferiority, shoddiness, the easy way out in development. Instead, he says he considers his greatest legacy to be introducing outstanding architects to the investment-building world. "Through that, we will build better cities," he says.

At the time it was completed, One Shell Plaza became the largest reinforced concrete building in the world, transforming the skyline of Houston and the career of Gerald Hines. The Galleria? Surprising, shocking, and successful beyond belief. "There was Galleria I and Galleria II and Galleria III, the whole neighborhood, and the extension down Post Oak Boulevard," says John Duncan. "It set off an expansion boom!" Gerald Hines' mother, Myrtle McConnell Hines—who lived to be one hundred years old—and father, Robert Hines, flew in from Gary for the grand opening. Seeing the Galleria, with its soaring glass barrel vault, its ice rink, its stores presented like jewel boxes with all

Hines developed such a reputation for fiscal integrity that he was appointed chairman of the Texas branch of the Federal Reserve Board under President Carter. His board medallion, below.

A reflective Hines in his office in the 1970s in front of a painting by Kenneth Noland. His accomplishments came quickly in this period, when he developed Shell's new headquarters and the Galleria simultaneously. It was at this time—he had personally guaranteed the construction costs of both the Galleria and Shell—that Hines decided to change his business structure, bringing in equity partners on future developments.

of Houston—and most of Texas—standing gape-mouthed in astonishment, Myrtle McConnell Hines turned to her son.

"Now, Gerry, you're not getting too far extended are you?" she asked.

Hines laughs now as he recounts the story. "That was already past," he says. "I had already done that."

■ ■ ■ ■ ■

With his survival came a new business plan. "It was a pretty good strategy: to build an aesthetically interesting building that would attract other clients," says Hines. "One of our major tenants was the law firm of Baker Botts. One of their clients was Pennzoil, whose president, Hugh Liedtke, liked our building so much he asked if we would think about building one for them."

Enter Philip Johnson, the dean of American architecture. He and Hines were already working together on the Post Oak Central building in Houston. They were on a plane together when Hines spoke the words that would unleash Johnson's imagination. "I said, 'I really need a second major tenant.'"

"Well, why not two buildings?" asked Johnson.

"Nobody has ever put two buildings on a block in Houston before," Hines said.

"Let me show you," said Johnson, and he drew a sketch on the back of a napkin: two trapezoids in counterpoint. "And sure enough, it was all there," says Hines. With that, yet another Hines trademark was exhibited in the building that became Pennzoil Place: great architecture for

great value. After the decision was made to design a second tower, the Zapata Oil Company, an offshore drilling company for which Liedtke served on the board of directors, stepped forward to claim the second building.

Of his relationship with Johnson, Hines recalls that it "started out a little antagonistically." It began with some differences of opinion on a Houston office building campus called Post Oak Central, which Hines had commissioned Johnson to design. "But he came to respect us and our knowledge," Hines adds. Soon, the two men, the architect and his Medici, would become indelibly bound. In 1975, legendary

Gerald Hines at the groundbreaking ceremony for Pennzoil Place, December 8, 1972. With him are Albert Woodcock (far left) and Paul Woodcock (next to Hines), owners of the antique oil rig transported from Pennsylvania to Houston to break ground at the event, and William C. Liedtke Jr. (second from left) of Pennzoil. The developer collects the hard hats he has worn while visiting project sites, and displays them in his Houston office. One piece in his collection is the hard hat he wore during the groundbreaking (inset), which still has his name Dyno-embossed on it.

New York Times architecture critic Ada Louise Huxtable named Pennzoil Place the Building of the Year. In the roaring 1970s, it came to represent the spirit of boomtown Houston. Pennzoil Place was 100 percent leased when it opened, while Houston was suffering with one-and-a-half to two million square feet of vacant office space.

"For the first time, office developers started moving to quality design," Johnson's partner, John Burgee, told a reporter. "We've actually had developers call us and keep asking, 'How does Hines do it?' Part of hiring us was to get into the mind of Gerry Hines."

Most developers would have arrived at the opening of a landmark building like Pennzoil Place in a limousine. Hines took his own car to the opening and ran out of gas on the way to the event. Without money for a fill-up, he had to call his secretary to dispatch an associate with petty cash. "I can't believe the poor man didn't have enough money to get gas," his then-secretary, Olga Turner, laughs.

Hines and Johnson collaborated on fifteen buildings across the United States, from Houston's landmark Transco Tower to the oval "Lipstick Building" at 53rd At Third in Manhattan to Franklin Square in Washington, D.C. "Everything I've done and everything I've been, I owe to Gerry Hines," Philip Johnson once said. The buildings they did together, and Hines buildings in general, have stood the test of time.

"Gerry's buildings are the kind that people pass and say, 'Wow,'" says John Duncan. "They are not conventional, but they have quality. When Houston was going through bad times because of office vacancies, Gerry's buildings were full."

On a plane ride with architect Philip Johnson, Hines said, "I really need a second major tenant" for the Pennzoil Place project, opposite. Johnson replied, "Well, why not two buildings?" and drew a sketch of two trapezoids in counterpoint on the back of a napkin. The new design cost less than the fifty-story building originally planned, and the project was 100 percent leased when it opened, amid high vacancy rates in the city. Right, early construction on Pennzoil Place.

Although his buildings were increasingly stylish and powerful, Hines remained, in many ways, the opposite. "Gerry occasionally stammered in contrast to being glib, and his presentation was full of way too many details," banker Ben Love once said about Hines' pitch to build the seventy-five-story headquarters of Texas Commerce Bank. "But he was so open and honest that the board voted unanimously to give him the project. They felt they could trust him."

Not everything has been a home run, of course. In 1979, Hines and his partners had just opened a Warwick Hotel on Post Oak near the Galleria. But then hyperinflation rendered the budget inadequate, loan rates soared to 16 percent, and the peso devaluation halted upscale Mexican travel to Houston and other American cities. All of this meant a very large loss would be looming on the project, both to Hines' company and Hines personally. When an associate, Gary Beck, nervously broke the news of the steep losses, he expected Hines to rant and rave. But the developer merely stared out the window and calmly said, "I never dreamed that I would be so fortunate to be able to afford to lose so much."

■ ■ ■ ■ ■

A visionary, Hines saw the future of his company early.

"Gerry used to often write me memos," says Perry Waughtal, who served as Hines' chief financial officer. "He'd wake up at three in the morning and dictate his thoughts and his ideas. The title of one memorandum was 'Dreams.' In that memo, he talked about how he saw the future of this company. Here we were, about a dozen people, struggling to try to get a major project off the ground, buying land for what would become the Galleria. And this memo said, 'Someday, we're going to have

offices all over the world. We're going to build major buildings in all the major cities, and this is how I think the company will be structured.' He went into great detail as to how the profit centers would be set up, where the offices would be—and so much of that came true."

In his personal life, Hines is equally gung ho, no limits, full steam ahead. "We went on a ski trip, where he went up to the instructor and said, 'We want to go in the intermediate class'—and he'd never skied," remembers Dorothy Hines. "He goes at everything with full enthusiasm and with full throttle."

His days typically began at 4:30 in the morning, says his daughter Jenny Hines Robertson. "He would go out jogging and I'd wake up at 5:30 to greet him in the kitchen after his run," she says.

Nov-19-1973-2:45 P.M.

Hines' enthusiasm for recreational activity—golf, skiing, mountain climbing, biking, and the like—is as robust as his passion for work. He became an avid mountain climber in the 1970s. The *Houston Chronicle Sunday Magazine* headline, above, reads: "The mountains some men climb—Gerald Hines' are as often real as steel." At right, the seventy-nine-year-old Hines plays at the firm's development, Palencia, in May 2004.

"When my mother had something to do in the morning, it would be Dad's duty to take me to school," remembers Jeff Hines. "He always left very early, and we'd often walk construction sites on the way. He certainly had strong time commitments, but he was a very good father."

He was at work at least by 6:00 each morning, refusing to delegate, handling everything from pitching new clients to negotiating leases to personally choosing the menu for the Galleria's new hotel. "My crazy days," he'd later describe the years before he learned to delegate. In 1975, at fifty, he went in for a routine physical before a climbing expedition in the Italian Dolomites, and the doctors suggested an angiogram. The test showed that his arteries were dangerously constricted.

Hines refused the surgery, vowing instead to fight his disease through diet and exercise. Guided by Dr. Bill Owen, a doctor in Houston, Hines went to Pritikin, the California longevity center and spa known for its mostly vegetarian diets. When he returned, he was a changed man. Over the next several years, he threw himself into diet and fitness with the same single-minded focus he had applied to business.

After twenty-eight years of marriage, Gerald and Dorothy Hines were amicably divorced.

In 1981, Hines married a woman who shared his passion for design and architecture, Barbara Fritzsche. She had been a design student at Pratt Institute in Brooklyn, New York, and would go on to

work as a painter. Her grandfather, Otto Hermann Fritzsche, was a real estate developer who helped rebuild post–World War II Berlin. He is remembered for several architectural innovations, such as the garden apartment and underground parking. When Gerry and Barbara met, she was working as a foreign language teacher in Düsseldorf, Germany.

They were married in a small family ceremony in Aspen, Colorado.

"He used to have five reels going at one time. Then he learned to meditate," says Barbara Hines. "He had to change from a Type A to a Type B person." He found a young doctor, Dean Ornish, who would go on to fame as an author, speaker, and healer. But back then, he was just out of Harvard, and Hines was one of the first patients to support his theory that heart disease can be reversed through diet, meditation, yoga, and aerobics. It worked. He built up his collateral arteries and embarked on a now-legendary regimen of diet and exercise.

His commitment to fitness is best exhibited in Aspen, where he's had a home since the 1950s. He and Barbara spend part of each year in their Charles Moore–designed home, which sits at the confluence of two rivers. Here, he embarks on hiking, mountain biking, skiing, rollerblading, and mountain climbing expeditions. Joined by fellow adventurers half his age, he routinely passes them by bike, hiking boot, and snowshoe. He's taken his company's associates on expeditions around the world. "No one on the Hines ski trip will ever forget Gerry coming off a glacier with a hard wind and snow in his face, at the end of a very long day, pushing himself forward to reach our singular destination in the open spaces of the Alps," remembers Hines associate Tommy Craig.

In 1981, Hines married Barbara Fritzsche, a painter who shares his passion for design and architecture. Above, the newlyweds leave their wedding in Aspen. Left, at sixty, Hines became a father for the second time, first with daughter Serena, who turned twenty-one in 2006; and with son Trevor, who turned twenty in 2006.

His transformation was not just physical. He also employed the help of a variety of meditation masters, most notably the late Sri Swami Satchidananda, one of the most revered yoga masters of all time, who would fly into Houston to teach Gerald Hines yoga—although they didn't call it that. "He was way ahead of his time—this is going back twenty-five years," says Barbara Hines. "When I would tell friends he was doing yoga, he would say, 'No, Barbara, call it "stretching,"' because he didn't want people like the bankers to think Gerry Hines was some wacky airhead that did yoga."

Once again, it worked.

"He became the master of his mental processes, instead of getting agitated about things," says Barbara Hines. "He still meditates morning and evening, which has helped him tune out the extraneous and stay focused."

At sixty, Hines became a father for the second time, first with Serena, who turned twenty-one in 2006 and is married to high-tech entrepreneur David Steinberg, whom she met when both were undergraduates at Yale. Son Trevor, who turned twenty in 2006, completed a year of rabbinical studies at Yeshiva Tiferes Bachurim in Morristown, New Jersey, and began undergraduate study at Yale. Trevor's interest in Judaism triggered a series of revelations—most notably that he had two Jewish grandmothers on his mother's side. This resulted in his sister and mother also returning to their Jewish roots, which had been suppressed during the anti-Semitic climate of pre–World War II Germany, and dramatically changed the direction of the Hines family's life. "What a great sport Gerry has been, supporting us in honoring the Sabbath and Jewish holidays and keeping a kosher kitchen," which, says Barbara Hines, "is not always easy."

Gerry Hines (center) with son Jeff (right) and Ken Shuttleworth, a prominent architect, in London. Jeff Hines joined his father's business in 1981 after graduating from Williams College and Harvard Business School. In 1990, he was appointed president.

"We didn't have any great plan," Hines says as the plane begins its descent into London. "No, it was just evolving plans and new opportunities opening, which opened up a new sector."

Prudent, practical, precise, refusing to make decisions in his head without the slide rule, Hines approached expansion into Europe with the same careful study and analysis with which he'd entered his other ventures. In the late 1980s, before the company had made a commitment to international expansion, Hines was presented with an opportunity to develop what would become Canary Wharf, a massive new mini city on the edge of London. Hines went to check it out. Immediately, Hines detected "the fatal flaw," his son Jeff remembers. "Dad has never been about being the biggest or the largest. It's about the quality of doing the right project. He called me from London, and I was surprised when he said, 'It's not the right project. It doesn't have the transportation infrastructure.'"

The Toronto-based development firm Olympia & York Developments Ltd., run by

the Reichmann brothers, accepted the deal, buying a Gulfstream to commute between Toronto and London and housing fifty thousand workers to begin construction, which would eventually cost $7 billion. After pumping in $3 billion of their own funds into the project, the Reichmanns went bankrupt. Their firm was decimated, and by 1993, according to *Forbes*, Canary Wharf stood "half empty, a twenty-first-century ghost town on the edge of London, and the family's vast $10 billion fortune is gone, consumed by real estate speculation and disastrous stock market investments." (By the time Hines was approaching its fiftieth anniversary in 2007, the Reichmann brothers had made a comeback and were involved in many large, successful development projects.)

By the early 1990s, when he felt the time was right, Hines went global. Business exploded, just as it had done in Houston and then across the United

States. He was the first American developer to rebuild in Berlin after unification, and he would lead the way of modern development in myriad other countries. "My grandfather would have been thrilled to see Gerry working in Berlin in such a grand way," says Barbara Hines.

In 1990, Jeff Hines was appointed president of the firm. He joined his father's business in 1981 after graduating from Williams College and Harvard Business School and marrying Wendy Jones in 1980. In 1991, Hines opened its first overseas office in Berlin, and business began to mushroom. "When the Iron Curtain came down, Gerry went over there and left his business card and his little-boy look in every city in Eastern Europe," Duncan told a *Denver Post* reporter in 1996. "Now, he's bombarded with opportunities."

Barbara, born in Germany and raised in Australia, wanted their children to have a European upbringing. By 1995, with projects in Moscow, Berlin, Paris, and beyond, Hines decided to follow the action in Europe, and asked his son Jeff to run the company from Houston. He and Barbara and the two children they had

Hines with his extended family at an award ceremony, above, and the Dalai Lama, left. The developer has met an array of notable figures in every corner of the globe during his career, but places a priority on family and friends. In 2006, Hines was working with a shipbuilder in Southampton, England, to realize a lifelong dream of building his own sailboat. Opposite, Hines taking a demonstration sail off the coast of St. Martin.

together, Serena, then eleven, and Trevor, then nine, lived in Estee Lauder's home on Eaton Square, loaned to them by their friends Leonard and Evelyn Lauder, while renovating their own house nearby.

Gerald Hines, Indianan-turned-Texan, became a citizen of the world. "At first, he thought everything about London was arduous," says Barbara Hines. "But in the third year, I remember we were back in Aspen in August, watching the latest James Bond film, which was set in London. He looked at me after the film and said, 'I miss London. I can't wait to get back.' I thought, 'Wow. The tide has turned.' He really enjoys Europe. He loves the action. He likes the fact that he can do business in five countries in one week with very little effort. He appreciates the cultures, and how everybody speaks several languages. When we have a dinner party, if there are ten people at the table, we have at least twenty countries represented, because everybody is from more than one country."

Soon, Hines was in almost every country at once, opening offices in Beijing in 1996, followed by projects in Spain, Italy, Germany, Mexico, the United Kingdom, France, Poland, Brazil, and Russia, and setting up partnerships with locals in the far-flung lands. "We have had very good partners in Russia, Italy, Germany, France, and Spain," says Hines. "Each of these countries has a different culture, and you have to have natives run those businesses. Selecting really great people is the key to our success. That's the number-one factor—people—and making sure you have creative plans to compensate them and let them participate in the success of the projects that they do."

He is still hot for the chase, indefatigable, inspiring action, traveling nonstop whenever and wherever he senses opportunities to advance Hines as the go-to developer for multinational corporations.

"His energy for the business has gone up," says E. Staman Ogilvie, executive vice president of Hines in Eurasia. "After Serena's wedding at the Villa Ephrussi de Rothschild in the South of France, while everyone else was still asleep, he and I boarded his plane and flew in darkness through the night to Bombay, where we jumped in a cab and went to our first meeting. What an enormous vibrancy he has, and what an example he sets for everyone. The essence of the man is he likes things that are new, and it engages him intellectually and viscerally to pursue that which has never been done before."

"The joy of work is the continuation of the learning process," Hines has said. And this is what is at the core of his nature: embracing everything that he finds "interesting," and following it wherever it leads, from Gary, Indiana, to practically every corner of the world.

In 2005, Gerald Hines turned eighty, and he was honored in Aspen by his interconnected worlds of development, architecture, finance, friendship, and family. His buildings are his legacy, but the man and his principles are at the foundation of each one. "Well, people need to be housed," he says as the plane lands. "Man has been building since the beginning of time to shelter himself. We just have to find ways to build that affect the ecology less and design for more efficient energy use. Focus our attention on 'green' buildings. As an engineer, that is very dear to my heart."

■ ■ ■ ■ ■

There are, of course, infinite tales of the buildings that arise in the wake of Hines and his company of three thousand

employees in more than one hundred offices on four continents—a multinational giant born of one man and a slide rule. But our flight is over, and, as always, Gerald Hines has to run.

I leave him in Heathrow Airport, where a car is waiting to take him to Southampton to meet with a shipbuilder, with whom Hines is realizing a lifelong dream of building his own sailboat. "When he turned eighty, he realized he'd better get on with it," Barbara Hines says. "He comes from a background of sea captains. That's in his blood. He wants to sail around the world with me when he gets his boat completed in a couple of years."

Does this mean retirement?

"Oh, he'll never retire," she continues. "He'll be on the boat and will get bored after two weeks, fly off, do some business, and then be happy to come back to his sailboat."

THE MAN
THE HISTORY
THE APPROACH
THE LEGACY

MODERNISM

2

Richmond
Avenue

Between 1957 and 1966, on a small stretch of Houston's Richmond Avenue, Gerald D. Hines Interests built fourteen modernist office buildings—the first of Hines' career. Twelve still stand, including 3323 Richmond, previous spread, a 12,000-square-foot elevated building by Neuhaus & Taylor, and 3101 Richmond Avenue, right.

Modernism Meets Richmond Avenue
by William Middleton

In 1992, Philip Johnson, who was in his late eighties and still hard at work, was sitting in his New York office discussing his extraordinary career. After reviewing the first few decades, the name of a certain real estate developer was slipped into the conversation. The architect and developer had worked together for twenty-five years, a remarkable collaboration that led to such important structures as the twin trapezoidal towers of Houston's Pennzoil Place; the nine-hundred-foot, sixty-four-story Transco Tower (now Williams Tower) near Houston's Galleria; and the elliptical 53rd At Third building (better known as the Lipstick Building) in Manhattan that housed his firm. Johnson looked out his office window, watching the traffic make its way up Third Avenue, and said, almost to himself, "Gerald Hines . . . where in the world did he come from?" ⊞ The short answer: a little stretch of suburban Houston called Richmond Avenue. It was on this leafy street, from 1956 through 1966, that Gerald D. Hines Interests built fourteen office buildings–the first of Hines' career. Twelve still stand, the earliest examples of Hines' work, in an area that has come to be known as the Richmond Corridor. As *Cite*, the architectural journal of the Rice Design Alliance, has put it: "The Richmond Corridor: Where Developer Gerald Hines Went to Graduate School." The Hines buildings here range from a simple 8,000-square-foot, one-story modernist structure, to a 22,000-square-foot, two-story building sheathed in black glass, to a stirring 58,000-square-foot, white travertine–clad mid-rise with a dramatic canti-levered penthouse. This collection of surprisingly sophisticated buildings, though most Houstonians aren't even aware of it, is where Gerry Hines got his groove.

The Richmond Corridor buildings are significant on several levels. The modernist structures, a total of twenty-nine built primarily by Hines and rival Century Development through 1971, represent one of the earliest examples of the suburban office park in the United States. In fact, early coverage of the area refers to it as "Office Park," then a novel term. "It could become Houston's first Modern Historic District," says Barry Moore, an architect and professor at the Gerald D. Hines College of Architecture at the University of Houston, who oversaw a recent architectural survey of the area. "The Richmond Corridor was the first concentration of commercial buildings outside of downtown," he explains, "and it was the hatching point for Gerald Hines. His buildings there set the stage for a completely different kind of developer in Houston, which then migrated across the country and throughout the world."

Stephen Fox, an architectural historian and professor at Rice University and the University of Houston, is also convinced of the area's significance. "Architecturally, it captures a moment in time," Fox says. "And the Richmond Corridor is important because it demonstrates Gerald Hines' emerging realization that distinctive architecture could be used to give buildings enhanced visibility and greater presence."

UNCOMPROMISING TASTE

Hines' awareness of the importance of good architecture is one of the most important lessons of these early buildings. "A building should have perpetual character and monumental quality," Hines explained to the *Houston Chronicle*, after

less than a decade in the business. And he made a case for the higher purpose of design. "In gaining maturity, Houston has all the opportunity to build a beautiful city," he said. "If our big corporations will be discerning and seek good architecture, we will achieve that beauty. Good design and good architecture upgrade a city and give it lasting beauty. The same amount of concrete and steel goes into a good or bad design."

From the very start, Hines seemed to be on a mission for the best. The headline on one of his first major profiles, published on the front page of the *Houston Chronicle* in 1967, was, "Gerald D. Hines' Goal: Everything a Little Better Than Anyone Else." He worked with some of the most respected architects in Houston, earning praise from the local and national design community. As A. Eugene Kohn, president of Kohn Pedersen Fox Associates in New York, has said, "He was the first developer in modern times to incorporate quality architecture. In the late 1940s, 1950s, and 1960s, a lot of development was less driven by quality and more driven by the bottom line. But Gerry Hines realized the value in designing buildings and workplaces that would make people proud—buildings they would want to show off."

Hines didn't advocate design for the sake of design, however. "We do not collect architecture," he once told *Architecture* magazine. "We use it. It is very utilitarian." He learned to have a pragmatic view of the benefits of architecture. "A well-designed building is the first to fill up—the main objective, after all—and the last to get vacated," he said in another publication.

Hines learned on Richmond that good design was marketable. Although the buildings gained plenty of attention for their

design, landscaping, and urban planning, some of the most important early praise Hines received was commercial. In 1967, he was named "Key Houstonian of the Year" by the Houston Board of Realtors, while in 1968, he was named "Marketing Man of the Year" by the Houston chapter of the American Marketing Association. As reported by the *Houston Post*, "Hines was cited for the use of outstanding design as a creative marketing tool in the development of successful office buildings."

There is another reason Hines focused early on good design: because he could. "I didn't have to worry about any skepticism about the cost because I was by myself," he explains. "I didn't have anyone criticizing me. We developed a good reputation and that's what was most important."

The Richmond buildings also helped Hines form an expansive view of his role as a full-service commercial developer. "We supervise the whole process, starting from the acquisition of the land, the market studies, the size of the project, how the project should look," Hines explained to the *Houston Chronicle*. "Then we determine which architect we think can get that kind of look that we want. . . . Then we have to determine our marketing strategy, how to lease space, then get the contracts to build the space, finance it, borrow the money, raise the equity if you can't borrow all the money . . . then bring in partners that own parts of it in addition to yourself. Then you supervise it through construction and leasing, and start property management of the building, which includes operation of the building once it's complete, plan for that and then execute it. And you continue to operate those properties through the life of the property." Hines concluded, the *Chronicle* noted, with a wry smile, "That's all the development business is."

John Duncan, who was the head of Gulf+Western Company and one of the first tenants of Gerald D. Hines Interests, has known the developer since his very first office on Richmond Avenue. "I knew Gerry Hines before he was the Gerry Hines," Duncan says with a laugh. He is convinced that Hines' arrival in the big leagues didn't come out of the blue. "It was an enormous jump," Duncan says of the move from the Richmond Corridor. "But he always did his homework. And he always had the guts to take the big jump."

Hines recalls those years with more understatement. "Well, I think that first we crawled, then we walked, then we jogged, and then we started to run," he says with his signature Midwestern modesty. "But in the crawling and walking stage was Richmond Avenue."

THE ROAD TO RICHMOND

At the time Gerald D. Hines Interests was getting off the ground, Houston was going through a remarkable post-war boom. The first major freeways were being constructed and new thoroughfares were being devised. By 1954, a street called Buffalo Speedway sliced across what had been farmland, connecting the elegant River Oaks neighborhood west of downtown with West University, the residential neighborhood west of Rice University and the Texas Medical Center. "That whole sector had been a void," points out Fox. "There were no buildings to the east, west, north, or south. So the opening of Buffalo Speedway in the 1950s was a big deal. The initial installation of buildings, led by the Humble Research Center and completed in 1954, gave that sector an identity."

The severe, fortress-like façade of 2990 Richmond, Hines' final building and largest up to that time on Richmond Avenue. The six-story, 90,000-square-foot building, designed by architects Neuhaus & Taylor, was built in 1966.

While the Humble Research Center, a sprawling modernist structure that is now the Exxon Research Center, helped give the area a commercial identity, Richmond Avenue became the focus of attention. In the late 1950s, once Richmond was punched through the undeveloped land, it became a perfectly placed, east-west thoroughfare. Connecting downtown with the western suburbs, it was positioned halfway between River Oaks and U.S. 59, a major highway from downtown to the southwest. The wide avenue, with a spacious landscaped esplanade, was lined with tropical plants, pines, and rows of live oak trees. As Hines remembers, "We could see that Richmond was going to be a very major street—and with the esplanade, a more dominant street—so we decided that we would try to accumulate land there."

Hines' first development deal marked his entry onto Richmond Avenue. It was a one-story, 5,000-square-foot office/warehouse for industrial instrumentation manufacturer Fischer & Porter at 3783 Richmond. The small building, with the office in the front and warehouse in the back, was designed by Neuhaus & Taylor—a leading Houston firm with which Hines would build six more projects on Richmond. The one-story Fischer & Porter building has since been demolished, as has the firm's second effort on Richmond: the Ingersoll-Rand building, a 25,000-square-foot office/warehouse at 4211.

As his firm continued to build bigger office/warehouses in outlying areas, including a 250,000-square-foot building for Western Auto in Dallas, Hines concentrated his office efforts on the five or six blocks at the eastern end of the Richmond Corridor. In 1959, he built the Prudential Insurance Company of America building, a one-story, 8,000-square-foot structure at 2929. The simple, modernist structure designed by Alan James features a flat roof, recessed entry, and large windows hidden behind a masonry block wall. It became the second office for Gerald D. Hines Interests.

In 1961, next door to the Prudential Building at 2903, Hines built a two-story, 16,000-square-foot office building for Gulf+Western. Now called the Friden Building (after its second tenant), it is a long, rectangular box with two stories of windows in front divided by a mesh screen running the length of the building. "The screen wall at the midpoint between the floors was designed to provide shade for the ground level," says J. Victor Neuhaus III, who, with his partner, designer Harwood Taylor, was one of Hines' closest collaborators on Richmond. "There is an overhang on top that provides shade for the second floor. At that point, reflective glazing and other improvements in insulated glass had not been developed, so a lot of our buildings had mechanical devices like overhangs and screens to keep the sun off the glass. The more glass that was exposed directly to the sun, the greater the demands on the air conditioning."

That same year, Hines called on Neuhaus & Taylor to create a striking building for the Pontiac Motor Division at 3121 Richmond. It is a 10,000-square-foot, flat-roofed structure raised up on steel columns, with ground-level parking for guests and employees. The roof has a wide overhang, shading the floor-to-ceiling glass of the second floor, while the ground floor has an all-glass entrance vestibule with a cantilevered stairway. With its pure International Style, the Pontiac building earned lots of attention. *Architectural Forum* compared it favorably with the Bacardi headquarters in Mexico City by Ludwig Mies van der Rohe. And the purity of the design has helped the building age gracefully. "I like the dramatic cantilevered roof and the freestanding columns," says University of Houston's Barry Moore. "It's a very elegant Harwood Taylor design—it looks like a pavilion in an oasis."

AN ELEVATED CONCEPT

Elevating the structure was an ingenious design for a small piece of land. "Instead of building on only half the lot, we were able to double the amount of parking and double the amount of leaseable area," remembers Vic Neuhaus. "So it was the best way to get additional area, and it provided covered parking, which in Houston is also a plus." The building's novel solution to the parking problem was another reason for its success. "The first-floor-for-cars, second-floor-for-people arrangement is a practical, economic concept," *Architectural Forum* noted. "People in suburban Houston—as in all suburbs—travel in cars; employees and customers come wrapped in six-by-sixteen-foot steel packages, so a large amount of parking space must be provided, and it is cheaper to lift a building off the ground and park under it than to purchase additional land for a parking lot. . . . And any building that retains its clarity while standing over a herd of cars has achieved a great deal."

Also in 1961, Hines built another striking structure for the Fireman's Fund Insurance Company at 3015 Richmond. The 22,000-square-foot, two-story building is a long rectangular box covered with white marble at either end and fronted

with a two-story curtain wall of black glass. The minimal design was by Lloyd, Morgan & Jones, which was also responsible for such notable Houston buildings as the twenty-five-story headquarters of American General Life Insurance. The first building on Richmond with a curtain wall, the sleek façade is broken only by a steel entrance canopy that juts out from the building.

"The best story about the Fireman's Fund building," recalls Louis Sklar, former executive vice president at Hines, "is an example of one innovation that failed. The building originally had, for aesthetic purposes, a sunken front parking lot. It, of course, flooded during a major rainstorm, so was filled in and paved—as it remains today."

Vic Neuhaus advises a member of his design team. With his partner, Harwood Taylor, he formed Neuhaus & Taylor, the Houston design firm with which Gerald Hines built seven projects on Richmond Avenue.

Hines built the 3000 Richmond building, designed by Wilson, Morris, Crain & Anderson, for Union Texas Petroleum in 1964. The five-story, 100,000-square-foot building featured bold columns of poured concrete and narrow slits of dark windows. Inside, it featured a refined lobby with terrazzo floors and glistening white marble walls.

Hines built 3015 Richmond, top, in 1961 for the Fireman's Fund Insurance Company. The following year, Hines built two more elevated structures on Richmond. The Pacific Indemnity Company, at 3118, middle, was an 11,000-square-foot building designed by Wilson, Morris, Crain & Anderson, with an office on the ground floor, a staircase up to the main space on the second floor, and parking below. The Richmond-Eastside Building, at 3101 Richmond, bottom, was a Neuhaus & Taylor design.

In 1962, Hines built two more elevated structures on Richmond. The Pacific Indemnity Company building, at 3118, was an 11,000-square-foot building designed by Wilson, Morris, Crain & Anderson, another well-respected Houston firm. The long, rectangular box has an office on the ground floor with a staircase up to the main space on the second floor, and parking below.

More remarkable is the Phoenix of Hartford Insurance Company building, at 3323 Richmond. This 12,000-square-foot elevated building by Neuhaus & Taylor has exuberant arched shades that curve up and out over the black glass of the second-floor offices. Although the form of the building is classic, the remarkable parabolic shades make it one of the most playful buildings on the street. Part pop art, part minimalist sculpture, it is also very practical. "Those screens were a function of trying to shade the glass," Vic Neuhaus explains. "No matter how much air conditioning you had, if someone was sitting next to a window, that person would be uncomfortable. So we always had to come up with some way to shade the glass."

Also in 1962, Hines built the Richmond-Eastside Building at 3101 Richmond. Although not large, this two-story, 21,000-square-foot building, again by Neuhaus & Taylor, was the most monumental building yet. The flat-roofed structure with a crisp overhang is clad in travertine with narrow strips of black windows that run the height of the building. The two-story entrance hall is a soaring affair with terrazzo floors, white marble walls, and a cantilevered staircase.

This elegant structure housed the next office, and third Richmond Avenue address, for Gerald D. Hines Interests.

MOVIN' ON UP
Across the street, in 1963, Hines built its first mid-rise, the 3100 Richmond building. This imposing five-story, 58,000-square-foot structure, designed by Neuhaus & Taylor, has an exterior of travertine with black vertical windows designed to echo the smaller building across the street. A dramatic cantilevered roof seems to float above the top floor, which originally housed the offices of Neuhaus & Taylor. "At that time, Gerry had his offices across the street in that two-story building that had a similar design," Neuhaus remembers. "We decided to pick up on the basic vertical elements so that the two would complement one another. Then we treated the upper floor, design-wise—with the cantilevered roof and the floor-to-ceiling windows—more like a penthouse."

The following year, Hines built the 3000 Richmond building for Union Texas Petroleum. This five-story, 100,000-square-foot building is a severe design by Wilson, Morris, Crain & Anderson that features bold columns of poured concrete and narrow slits of dark windows. The refined lobby features terrazzo floors, glistening white marble walls, and a pair of elevators behind stainless steel doors. It was built to hold 350 employees of Union Texas and other divisions of Allied Chemical.

In 1965, Hines built the Addressograph-Multigraph Corporation building at 2900 Richmond. This utilitarian, two-story, 30,000-square-foot structure—also by Wilson, Morris, Crain & Anderson—is rectangular with curving walls of pale red brick and narrow columns of dark windows.

In 1966, next door to Addressograph-Multigraph, Hines constructed his final building in the area, 2990 Richmond. The six-story, 90,000-square-foot structure, also by Neuhaus & Taylor, was Hines' largest office to date. It is another severe design, suggesting Brutalism was in the architectural air, in pale brick and black glass. Concern was given, however, to its context. "The building was designed to provide architectural continuity with the adjacent buildings," noted *Texas Architect*. "The curved brick masonry walls echo the building to the east, while the vertical window fenestration and fin walls blend with the building to the west of this structure." The structure was raised up almost six feet, which managed to soften the design.

The interiors of the Richmond Avenue office buildings that Hines designed in the 1960s were as modern as their sleek façades. Above, the lobby of the 3100 Richmond building.

A MODEL FOR OTHERS

This ensemble of Hines buildings speaks volumes about modern architecture and real estate development. "The Richmond Corridor shows how developers worked with architects to reach solutions to the

A watercolor rendering of 2990 Richmond Avenue. In 1966, Neuhaus & Taylor designed what would be Gerald Hines' last building for the Richmond Corridor. Clad in pale brick, "the building was designed to provide architectural continuity with the adjacent buildings," noted *Texas Architect*.

NEUHAUS & TAYLOR

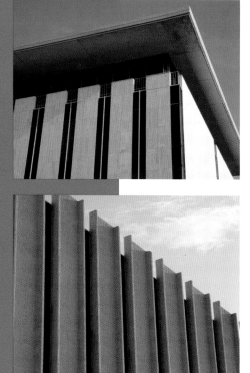

practical problems they had to confront," says architectural historian Fox. "And these buildings addressed the problem of reproducing the same structure over and over again but in a way that seemed distinctive."

Moore and Anna Mod, an architectural historian and project coordinator for the Richmond Corridor architectural survey, point to other technical innovations in the buildings. "Richmond was the testing ground for features that are now common: the full-height solid-core door; the integrated aluminum door-and-frame system; stainless steel lever hardware; nine-foot ceilings," Moore and Mod wrote. "Here also were the proving grounds for the thirty-three-foot lease depth, which accommodated small tenants, and for mullions spaced every five feet along the windows, a standard that made space planning easier."

As Hines suggests, "Those buildings on Richmond prepared me for the later buildings, in terms of understanding the desires of tenants and all of the systems. They helped us learn about the type of flexibility I wanted to build into a building. When we built Shell, we found out that they changed approximately 30 to 35 percent of their space every year. We were able to give them a building and a system where they could cut that cost of moving people around by about 70 percent. Because of what we had done before, we were able to provide a very low operating cost and low cost of reconfiguration."

The success of the Richmond Corridor came from the same factors that have driven suburban development across the nation: lower rents compared with downtown, convenient parking, and proximity to residential neighborhoods. "It was also the first time that there was a large inventory of modest office buildings, so that a smaller tenant could have building recognition," says Moore. "With a 12,000-square-foot project, you could have your name on the building, which you couldn't do downtown."

Moore, who in addition to being on the faculty at the University of Houston is also a second-generation Houston architect, calls attention to Hines' evolution of priorities. "If you look at those buildings chronologically, you can see his developing attention to the places that make the biggest difference to tenants and prospective tenants," Moore explains. "There is a very high level of materials and finish in the lobby, elevators, and restrooms—the places people see and touch the most."

Moore also suggests that there were commercial factors for the design solutions to the harsh Houston sun. "Harwood Taylor was always experimenting with ways to cut down on air conditioning," Moore says of the designer of Neuhaus & Taylor. "Before it was an energy issue, or an ecological issue, it was a marketing issue for Hines. If you could cut down on costs you could save money for tenants and reflect that in the rate."

Another Hines innovation on Richmond was that he leased the land rather than buying it outright. "Long-term land leases allowed Hines to develop in a very different way," Moore explains. "In Houston, you hadn't done that before—you always had to buy the land. Leasing allowed him to use his money in a better way, and he developed ways to turn that to his advantage. By 1970, that's the way everyone wanted to do things."

And Richmond Avenue was the setting for something else: a good, old-fashioned real estate rivalry. In 1961, once Hines had begun concentrating on the eastern blocks of Richmond, Kenneth Schnitzer and his company, Century Development, started building to the west. Century built more than a half dozen significant structures on Richmond, and by 1966 controlled a huge parcel of land on the western section of the corridor. It was here that Schnitzer built Greenway Plaza, now an expansive development with 4.2 million square feet of office space in ten major buildings, ranging from eleven to thirty-one stories. "I think what Hines was doing on Richmond helped stimulate Greenway Plaza," says Moore. "Because Schnitzer was a talented developer as well and he wanted to get in on the same thing Hines was doing. I think one of the reasons Hines catapulted over to the Galleria is that Schnitzer blocked him in on the chessboard when he acquired the forty acres that became Greenway Plaza. Hines realized there wasn't any game left on Richmond and went over to the Galleria."

In 1969, Hines completed Post Oak Tower (now 5051 Westheimer), a twenty-two-story, 375,000-square-foot office building on the West Loop, part of a new interstate highway that circled the city, adjacent to the Galleria. In 1970, he opened the first phase of the Galleria, the 600,000-square-foot mall. The following year, One Shell Plaza opened downtown, a fifty-story, 1.2 million-square-foot building that became the tallest concrete structure in the world. Once Post Oak Tower had opened, Gerald D. Hines Interests moved its office there, leaving Richmond Avenue for good.

As Hines has taken on bigger and bigger projects around the globe, the dozen structures on Richmond have all been sold.

The buildings in the Richmond Corridor are like the first notes of a work that would go on to be an international triumph: an overture to a magnum opus. They are the earliest suggestions, though not well known today by the general public, of a success that now seems obvious. "After those projects, I think it was inevitable that he would grow," Barry Moore points out. "Hines was so successful at the small buildings that if two were good, then five would be better. And if five were better, then how about fifty?"

3

While developing a
freestanding store for
a department-store
chain, Hines noticed
several open parcels of
land on the southwest
corner of Post Oak
and Westheimer, about
seven miles from
downtown Houston. It
would become the site
of the Galleria. Here,
the hotel portion of
the Galleria in Houston
during construction.

GALLERIA

The Galleria Vittorio
Emanuele II in Milan,
inspiration for the
Houston Galleria. Built
in 1867, that Galleria is
two intersecting streets
of multistory, mixed-
use buildings, with an
iron-and-glass roof
stretching over them.
Hines was inspired
by the experience of
strolling under the
central glass skylight.

In the early 1960s, John F. Kennedy was president, Elvis was the rage, suburban America was booming, and developers were taking note of a new project called Southdale Center in Edina, Minnesota, the first enclosed mall in the U.S. It was in this era, and early in his career, that Gerald Hines noticed a prime piece of Houston real estate. He was in his thirties, and had declared himself a full-time developer only a few years before. He'd mainly built warehouses and small office buildings, most of them on less-than-prime land. But while developing a freestanding store for Joske's, a department-store chain, he became enraptured with some parcels of land on the southwest corner of Post Oak and Westheimer. ▉ Hines liked the area, about seven miles southwest of downtown, and thought it would be a good place for a shopping mall. But he had a different idea of what a suburban mall could be. ▉ That idea became the Galleria. The now-legendary mall/office/hotel mega-complex strained Hines' little organization and exposed the developer to a level of risk he'd never again accept. Other developers politely told him that the mall's unusual design was interesting—the plan called for four floors of shopping, an ice rink in the middle, and only one anchor store—but predicted that he'd have a tough time. He had trouble borrowing money. ▉ But Hines won his bet. The Galleria became wildly successful, luring not just shoppers from the nearby neighborhood but from throughout Texas and the Southwest—and even from Mexico and South America. Architecturally notable and luxurious, the project became a signature for Hines, proof of what he could do.

And over the years, the Galleria reshaped Houston, spawning development that amounted to a second downtown. The high-end neighborhood of shopping, office towers, hotels, and residential buildings now officially known as Uptown Houston is roughly the size of downtown Denver.

But it wasn't just Hines and Houston that the Galleria changed. It also reshaped shopping across the U.S. Throughout the 1970s, copies sprang up across the country. For a while it seemed that every ambitious shopping complex was upscale, multistoried, and enclosed by an atrium—many even sported ice rinks. Hines hadn't copyrighted the name "Galleria" outside of Texas, and other developers appropriated that, too. Gallerias appeared in Atlanta, Fort Lauderdale, and San Francisco—as well as in some less obvious shopping meccas like Poughkeepsie, New York, and Hoover, Alabama. "Going to the Galleria" became a craving for self-proclaimed "valley girls" as mall shopping became a permanent part of teen pop culture and designer goods took root in the rise of rampant consumerism.

Years later, an interviewer asked Hines if he'd anticipated the Galleria's impact. "No, no," he said. "Nobody can be that smart."

■ ■ ■ ■ ■

Let's begin where Gerald Hines began: with the location, location, location—the now-golden intersection of Westheimer and Post Oak Boulevard. In the early 1950s, it was nothing notable. Westheimer was a farm-to-market road, FM1028, lined with farms tended by Italian immigrants. When oilman Michel Halbouty built a one-story office there, he had to shell-and-tar the road in front. But Houston was growing fast—it had long since surpassed Dallas as Texas' largest city—and even before the 1970s oil boom, Houston had a moneyed air. By the late 1950s, developers had noticed that stretch of Westheimer and its proximity to River Oaks, the city's ritziest neighborhood, as well as swank up-and-coming enclaves such as Tanglewood, Briargrove, and Memorial. Planners called the area "the Magic Circle," and it grew even more magical in 1962, when the

Uptown Houston in 2006, including the Williams Tower, the Galleria, and the 610 Loop. The development of the Galleria reshaped the city of Houston, spawning development that created a second downtown. The high-end neighborhood of shopping, office towers, hotels, and residential buildings, now officially known as Uptown Houston, is roughly the size of downtown Denver.

Loop 610/Highway 59 interchange opened there. Drive time from downtown Houston dropped to less than fifteen minutes.

When Joske's, a regional department store, opened in 1963 just outside Loop 610, it shared the Westheimer/Post Oak intersection with a Weingarten's grocery store and Sakowitz, then the city's most expensive department store. But directly across from Joske's (now Dillard's), on the land that would become the Galleria, Westheimer lapsed into a hodgepodge of operations: Halbouty's office; Houston First Savings and Loan; Tony's, a Continental restaurant; a photography studio; a dance studio; and an antique store. Hines thought that area was a natural place for an upscale mall—something Houston didn't yet have. To assemble six or seven of those parcels of land, he lined up low-profile partners—individual Houstonians—to buy the land. He'd never acquired such a large, complicated parcel before, and he didn't enjoy the white-knuckle deal-making that stretched over nearly five years. "That's always the most frustrating, tense, least-fun job," he says. "That's the horrible part of the development business."

He started by making a "combination deal" with Houston First: he'd not only pay for the savings and loan's land, but would offer it the exclusive right to deliver banking services in the new mall. Halbouty signed on as a land-owning partner, and other complicated deals followed. The Berachah Church released some of its land with the proviso that church members could park on Hines' property on Sundays.

At one point, Hines controlled two hundred acres in the Post Oak area, thirty-three of which he needed for the mall

complex he planned. To an unusually large degree, Hines kept equity in his project—meaning that he'd keep more of the profits from a success, but that a failure would fall heavily on his small company. Observers called that strategy "a bold stroke" and "an expensive bet"—the sort for which Hines was later labeled "a wildcat developer." At a time when most shopping centers were built on land costing around 50 cents a square foot, this land averaged around $3.50.

"It was a huge risk," says Perry Waughtal, Hines' chief financial officer at the time.

"He was betting the plantation, like a riverboat gambler," says Louis Sklar, a retired Hines executive.

The pressure, Hines knew, was on.

An illustration of the Galleria exterior from the 1970s. Developers built a wave of distinctive enclosed malls during the 1950s and 1960s.

■ ■ ■ ■ ■

Malls live or die by their anchor stores, and Hines set his sights on a prime one: Neiman Marcus, the Dallas-based embodiment of Texas chic. The Marcus family was unhappy with their Houston store's downtown location, and like Hines, they'd decided that the future of Houston retailing lay to the west. But by the time Gerald Hines approached them, they'd already bought their own land: twenty-five acres on Westheimer, just inside the 610 Loop, a little closer to downtown than Hines' site. They were drawing up plans to build a freestanding store.

Hines had never met Stanley Marcus, the head of the chain, but he made an appointment, flew to Dallas, and introduced himself to the family—brothers Stanley, Lawrence, and Edward—at their office. Hines actually preferred to hold important meetings on someone else's turf, or at least at a neutral restaurant; his own small offices were unimpressive. At one point, a Houston client joked that he thought Hines worked out of his car.

The Marcuses, second-generation retailing royalty, had fashion and glad-handing in their blood. Hines was cut from different cloth. Passionate but slightly shy, he weighed around 140 pounds and his big tortoiseshell glasses matched the suits he gravitated toward. A slide rule was his most notable accessory. "He's the last fellow in the world I'd expect to be a real-estate developer," says Lawrence Marcus. "He looked more like a geologist."

But Hines' pitch to the Marcuses didn't rely on flash. It relied on money, and he was relentless in convincing them to join him and abandon the tract they'd already bought. Hines said that with his experience in Houston, he could have them operational in the suburbs faster than if they built on their own. If Neiman's joined him at the mall, he'd provide the land and infrastructure such as a parking garage. They could have the best spot, the high-visibility corner closest to the freeway. And the deal got even sweeter: "Part of the contract," remembers Lawrence Marcus, "was that Hines ended up paying us rent instead of our paying him. It was very attractive."

Ultimately, they agreed that Neiman's would construct its own building at the site. The Marcuses were already working with up-and-coming architect Gyo Obata. The soft-spoken Obata, then in his thirties, was a partner in Hellmuth, Obata + Kassabaum; his long design credits would eventually include major airports and the National Air and Space Museum in Washington, D.C. But though Obata had designed impressive, elegant buildings in St. Louis, where his firm was based, he'd only recently begun landing commissions outside that city. The Houston Neiman's, with its ambitious budget and high visibility, was a coup for the young designer.

Hines brought in Obata as the entire project's lead design architect to make the mall more consistent with Neiman's. As the local associate architects, Hines hired Neuhaus & Taylor, a firm that designed some of Hines' office buildings along Richmond Avenue. Their work included one of the largest buildings Hines had constructed at that point: 2990 Richmond

The Marcus family, of Neiman Marcus, assists at the official groundbreaking of the Galleria in July 1967, near right. Edward Marcus is at left with his back to the camera; Lawrence Marcus is facing the camera. Gerald Hines can be seen just to the right of Lawrence's head. Far right, construction at the Galleria site.

Avenue, a five-story office building. The Galleria was on an entirely different scale.

Relocating to Houston, Lawrence Marcus worked closely with Hines and Obata. He and Obata fondly recall traveling with Hines, looking at shopping centers in other parts of the U.S., trying to figure out how to make something more distinctive, cohesive, and elegant. Everywhere, says Marcus, Hines examined the buildings' details down to their doorknobs and hinges. And everywhere, he whipped out the slide rule he kept in his pocket. "He was always figuring out what a bulk order of a certain kind of hardware would cost," says Marcus.

■ ■ ■ ■ ■

Hines figured that to make money on his expensive land, he'd have to "intensify the use"—that is, extract more money per square foot than the usual mall could. Part of that would be accomplished by building parking garages instead of the huge surface lots that surrounded most malls of the era. In Houston, where much of downtown's parking was still on surface lots, the concept seemed especially radical.

But on top of that, Hines and Obata hatched a concept even more astounding: this mall wouldn't be just a mall. It would also contain a hotel and office tower.

In the trade, such combinations are called "mixed-use developments," and in the 1960s, they were generally considered relics of the past. Since the dawn of human construction, people had used buildings for more than one purpose: shopkeepers lived over their stores; kings conducted government business from their castles; farmers slept in the same buildings as their animals. But since the rise of the sleek International Style, most architects viewed mixed-use buildings as messy and inefficient. A house was supposed to be a machine for living; a mall, a machine for shopping; and so on. Mixing things up, the theory went, only yielded a muddle. In most cities, zoning laws and parking requirements enforced that line of thinking.

But Houston, with no zoning at all, was wide open to new ideas.

The revival of mixed-use development was generally seen as the sort of thing embraced by people who ate bean sprouts and railed against the corporate machine. In 1961, Jane Jacobs published the movement's bible, *The Death and Life of Great American Cities*, a book that seemed radical at the time. She pointed out that gigantic, new, single-use buildings, such as housing projects, often failed, quickly becoming centers of urban blight. She compared them to thriving, lively older neighborhoods, such as Greenwich Village, where she lived— places where people walked past several businesses on their way to work, where they enjoyed watching other people, where they felt safe, where they moved about at all hours for many different reasons. Cities, she argued, need "intricate and close-grained diversity of uses that give each other constant mutual support."

Obata designed the mall around a long atrium topped with a huge skylight, above. In selecting a management company for the ice skating rink, Gerald Hines turned to another great brand: Ice Capades. Left, Hines meets with Michael Kirby (right), manager of operations for Ice Capades, and George Eby (center), president of Ice Capades.

Hines quickly saw that mixing his development's uses made good economic sense. Combining the mall with a hotel and office would mean that the complex could generate business during all hours of the day, not just peak office hours. Shoppers tended to flock on weekends, when the office building was largely vacant; hotel guests were usually there for the night, not the day. By bringing in people other than shoppers, Hines could guarantee that his valuable parking spaces would be occupied more hours of the day. And hotel guests and office workers could shop and eat at the mall—an arrangement that counted as an amenity for the guests and office workers, and that offered merchants and restaurants a built-in pool of potential customers.

To intensify the space even more, he planned to build upward. The office building would be twenty-two stories; the hotel, twenty-one. Those buildings would have seemed tall in Houston's downtown, but in the suburbs they'd stand out even more. But most surprising, Hines planned to make the mall four stories tall. At the time, a mere three-story mall would have been considered radical; conventional wisdom held that shoppers were hard to lure off the main floor.

Obata designed the mall around a long atrium topped with a huge skylight. Other malls had built ice rinks before, but those rinks were off to the side, in smaller enclosed areas where it was cheaper to keep the ice chilled. This rink, though, would be smack in the middle of the mall, visible from every floor.

Earl Marchand, a Rice University–trained engineer, oversaw all construction on the Galleria. Extremely intelligent and detail-oriented, Marchand was the person who made sure that Houston's Galleria—and, later, Dallas' Galleria—was constructed with the exacting standards that Gerald Hines expected. Although Hines himself had a mechanical engineering background, it was Marchand who embodied the engineering stereotype, says Louis Sklar. "Earl was a very bright guy," recalls Sklar. "The joke around the office was that if you asked Earl the time, he would build you a watch."

Gerald Hines credits Marchand with the Galleria's successful completion, and with engendering the confidence of everyone involved in the project. "People believed and trusted Earl, because they knew he did his homework," says Hines.

Later, during the holiday season, the mall would install on the ice a giant Christmas tree that stretched to the top of the glass atrium. Skaters would delight in circling the alpine obstacle while throngs of shoppers and visitors would gather to admire the centerpiece of the shopping center at its holiday best.

The design only looked wildly extravagant. Though the 170-foot rink was directly below an equally huge skylight, exposed to the relentless Texas sun, high-tech glass would reduce the solar heat. Hines had calculated the extra cost of locating the rink at the center of the mall, with three stories of air above it. Against that cost, he balanced that the extra activity generated by the rink would make the mall's basement floor more attractive to tenants, who'd be willing to pay almost as much to be there as on the main floor.

Hines thought the rink would enliven the whole mall, making it feel like something more than a place to shop. He and Obata frequently said that they wanted their mall to be a gathering place—like Rockefeller Center in New York, or the Spanish Steps in Rome.

Invoking another European model, Hines proposed to call his development "the Galleria" after the Galleria Vittorio

Emanuele II in Milan. Built in 1867, that Galleria is really two intersecting streets with a glorious iron-and-glass roof stretching over them, connecting sumptuous multistory, mixed-use buildings. Shoppers stroll about, dry even during the rain. Hines admired the lively place, as had generations of Italians and tourists before him. "I should like to live in it all my life," Mark Twain wrote in A Tramp Abroad.

Not everyone liked the name. Hines' contact at Western International, the hotel chain that had agreed to operate the Galleria hotel (and became Westin Hotels & Resorts in 1980), said that the word—Italian for "gallery"—would be too hard for Texans to pronounce.

More unnerving criticism came from other developers. At one of the Urban Land Institute's national gatherings, Hines presented his plans to a room full of other developers and real estate professionals. They were not wowed. The ice-rink concept, they said, was "a nice idea" but not worth the leasable space it would occupy. They pointed out the weakness of a one-anchor mall; most malls had at least two, one on each end, to lure shoppers to walk back and forth, past all the shops in the middle. And four stories, they said, was too many.

■ ■ ■ ■ ■

Though Hines was betting big on the Galleria, it wasn't his only project. He'd been trying to work out a deal with Houston Natural Gas, but for reasons beyond his control, it fell apart. Shell Oil then offered Hines the chance to bid on an even bigger project: the skyscraper that would become the company's regional headquarters in downtown Houston.

Hines proposed a fifty-story building—it would be the tallest building in the South— with innovative poured-in-place concrete walls instead of structural piers. It would be designed by the nationally recognized Chicago architecture firm Skidmore, Owings & Merrill.

To almost everyone's surprise, Hines beat out the competing developers, many of them national firms. With Shell's commitment to lease office space, Hines was able to borrow $35 million to build One Shell Plaza, and his company, with just a small number of employees, now found itself occupied with not one but two gigantic projects. One Shell Plaza alone, notes Waughtal, "was twice the cumulative total of everything we'd done up until then."

Although the consummate entrepreneur, Gerald Hines relied on men like Waughtal and Bob Elder to keep the engine of a busy company going. When Louis Sklar joined the firm in 1968, the Galleria and One Shell Plaza were underway, and Elder was largely overseeing the development of One Shell. "Bob, in spite of not having a clear-cut assignment, really was the person who, by today's project operations standards, made that project happen," recalls Sklar. Like Hines, Elder had come from industrial sales: Elder was selling industrial pumps when Hines was in the air conditioning business. Gerald Hines felt very comfortable with Elder's ability to bring oversight to One Shell, says Sklar, and has acknowledged Elder as the glue that held that project together.

Gerald D. Hines Interests grew to roughly thirty employees, all stretched to their limits. "We worked around the clock," Waughtal remembers fondly. "We worked from 8:00 a.m. to 8:00 p.m. on weekdays and a half day on Sunday. We were executing Gerry's vision, and everything was so important: every contract, every construction deal. It was fun. As we got bigger, it was never as fun again. Nothing was ever that critical."

Proposed expansion of the Galleria, above, shows the retail levels with six stories of office space above. In 1973, the actual expansion, right, included a twenty-five-story office tower; the proposed fountain was scrapped, but rounded balconies were added. In 1977, the company opened Galleria II, a skylighted wing containing a Lord & Taylor anchor store, twelve-story twin tower financial centers, and a second hotel.

Lenders were dubious about the Galleria for all the same reasons developers were, and its financing was far harder to arrange than One Shell Plaza's. Instead of a single project loan, Hines had to bootstrap the Galleria, winning its loans in increments. Lenders deemed the office building the safest bet—Hines had a track record with those—so Hines started its construction first.

Neiman Marcus was responsible for its own building. But to finance the rest of the mall, Hines needed to show that he had tenants willing to lease it. To line up those tenants—and to provide his company with the retail experience it lacked—Hines hired an acquaintance from his Unitarian Universalist church: Robert Kaim, a German immigrant who had been the vice president in charge of hard goods at Foley's department store.

"I decided to apply the principles of a department store to the entire mall," Kaim told the *Houston Post* in 1990, a year before his death. From his extensive retail contacts, he composed a mix of merchants the same careful way a retailer chooses his wares. "The merchants that came in needed to attract a 'medium' to 'better' quality customer," he said, "have good identification, and be experienced enough to operate in this kind of complex." He told prospective tenants where they'd be located in the mall and how much space they should occupy—a level of control never before exercised at a mall.

Over time, Kaim and Hines lined up blue-chip tenants: upscale national retailers such as Gumps, Mark Cross, Tiffany & Co., and furniture store W. & J. Sloane.

The tony local Isabell Gerhart would be one of a dozen high-end clothing stores. By opening day, there would also be two movie cinemas, nine shoe stores, several gourmet stores and candy shops, and fifteen restaurants clustered around the ice rink. The third floor was Kaim's toughest challenge: everyone feared that it would have no foot traffic. There, he installed quiet, classy establishments, such as art galleries. But even Kaim couldn't line up tenants fast enough to suit the lenders. And the one that finally agreed to finance the mall provided funding for only three floors.

Reluctantly, Hines "capped off" the mall at three stories, but he left in the structure space for the fourth story, and wondered what he could do on the extra floor. Hines, a fitness buff, loved to play tennis, so the idea came to him naturally: "I said, 'By golly, we've got those thirty-by-thirty-foot bays—we'll put tennis courts up there.'" Those ten indoor tennis courts became a major selling point for memberships to the private sports and social club located in the Galleria. They were the first in Houston to be air-conditioned.

Hines' partners had grown used to radical ideas. When he presented his tennis-court idea, Ed Randall responded with something like resignation. "Thank goodness Gerry doesn't play golf," he said.

■ ■ ■ ■ ■

The mega-complex opened in stages. Neiman Marcus came first, in 1969. The building was sculptural, and critics loved the store's light and elegance. Shoppers arrived in throngs and it became the most successful of Neiman Marcus' stores.

Post Oak Tower opened soon after, and Hines' firm moved its offices to a high floor. On the seventeenth floor, Neuhaus & Taylor, the Galleria's Houston architects, also took up residence. In their new offices, the developer and architect could easily monitor the rest of the Galleria's construction. And from Gerald D. Hines Interests' twenty-first-floor windows, employees could also see One Shell Plaza rising downtown. It was an intoxicating view.

The mall portion of the Galleria opened on November 16, 1970. The mall was only 60 percent leased—many of those third-floor slots were dark—but it quickly proved doubters wrong. The newspapers gushed. Skaters happily paid $1.50 to glide on the ice, and tennis players flocked to the GrassTex courts of the University Club, open sixteen hours a day. Shoppers were astounded by the view upward through the skylight. You could see the hotel under construction, and sometimes you'd see a jogger chugging around the club's track.

"It was a landmark in the world of retailing," remembers Melvin Simon, founder of what would become the Simon Property Group. "It was the first mall to target luxury to that degree."

In December the *Houston Post* offered perhaps the strongest assessment of the Galleria's success. The mall attracted so many people that the freeway couldn't handle them. "At times," noted the *Post*, "traffic has been backed up on Westheimer, under the loop, up to the service road, and even onto the loop itself."

The Galleria was, by all measures, a hit. Its open slots were leased, and by March, Hines was already announcing plans to expand. "A shopping center it is not," Hines once said. "It will be a new downtown."

In an article that seems to encapsulate much of the 1970s, the *Houston Post* covered a Hines-sponsored conference on the future of projects like the Galleria. "The Galleria concept is too important to be developed solely by merchants," said Washington University sociologist Robert

Early artwork illustrates the variety of offerings on each level of the Galleria, opposite. Above, the Tiffany & Co. store exemplified the upscale tenants that were attracted to the landmark mall. High-end stores mingled harmoniously with moderate toy stores—and even the teens who came to hang out at the ice rink, left. Hines and Obata frequently said that they wanted their mall to be a community gathering place—like Rockefeller Center in New York, or the Spanish Steps in Rome.

Hines set a standard of lavish decorations and special events that drew Houston's most distinguished shoppers. Hines installed the largest indoor holiday trees on Galleria ice rinks, above top, Houston. Above bottom, Gerald Hines with Dee Osborne (center) and Sakowitz heiress Lynn Wyatt, a prominent Houston socialite and tastemaker.

Boguslaw. "It's an effort to create a feeling of humanity which is so conspicuously absent from so much of the current scene."

Hines was committed to lavish decorations and special events designed to activate the common area, draw shoppers, and entertain employees and visitors. A giant garden and flower show, Primavera, turned the center into a massive, lush greenhouse each year during the ten-day period before Easter. That holiday is one of the most important travel periods for high-end Mexican shoppers and, at one point, their spending accounted for up to 30 percent of the mall's sales. During the G7 Economic Summit in Houston in 1990, enormous flags from the participating countries flew in the Galleria's atrium, including the largest American flag ever displayed indoors, looming over three custom grand pianos—one each lacquered red, white, and blue. Three pianists delighted visitors with three-part renditions of beloved songs from the participating countries.

Galleria events were brought in on a budget and a schedule, but the emphasis was on being first-rate. Flowers couldn't be silk; they had to be fresh. At the mall's annual Christmas ice pageant, the day after Thanksgiving, the skaters' costumes were made of real velvet, with real sable on the collars. Music was provided by the Houston Grand Opera.

George Lancaster, Hines vice president of corporate communications, was director of marketing for the Galleria in the 1990s. "The Galleria was the cafeteria for all of the Houston Hines executives," Lancaster notes, "so we were very keen on keeping it pristine at all times. We all knew that Mr. Hines occasionally ventured into the mall to shop, and we knew he was extremely proud of the center. We all shared in that same pride in being number one. It propelled us."

The Galleria proved its success to everyone who'd once doubted it. In 1979, the Urban Land Institute—the same organization that had expressed resounding doubts about Hines' plans a decade earlier—awarded the project the institute's first-ever Award of Excellence. As shoppers, office workers, and hotel guests flocked to it, the Galleria grew and grew again, but Galleria I, as the original part of the mall is called, remains its elegant old self. The 1970s bronze fixtures have been replaced with more stylish chrome, and brown carpet has given way to marble floors, but skaters still glide across the ice rink, and the skylight still reveals the occasional jogger.

In spite of intense competition for retailers, the Galleria has never lost its lead as the preferred address for upscale retailing in Houston. The Galleria's commitment to identifying and leasing to important retailers has never wavered; significant inducement dollars have been put into this program, which has been key to maintaining the shopping center's market position.

Hines added a twenty-five-story office tower to the complex in 1973. In 1977, the company opened Galleria II, a skylighted wing containing a Lord & Taylor anchor store, twelve-story twin tower financial centers, and a second hotel. (By now Hines had clearly won the name game. Western International opened a second hotel in Galleria II .)

In 1986, Galleria III was completed, bringing anchors Saks Fifth Avenue and Macy's. For the opening of Galleria III, Macy's imported Tony Bennett, who gave a concert in the mall's center court.

The Houston Galleria remains the most popular mall in Texas, drawing nearly twenty-four million visitors a year. At 2.4 million square feet, it is the fifth-largest mall in the U.S. The Galleria's Neiman Marcus remains one of the chain's most profitable stores.

The Houston Galleria was so successful that Hines copied it in Dallas, where Obata designed yet another luxury mall with a skating rink. It opened in 1982 and included a Westin Hotel and multiple office towers. In 1999, Hines sold the Houston Galleria to Urban Retail Properties; the deal included the office towers, hotels, and some adjoining raw land. Soon after, Hines sold the Dallas Galleria as well.

So successful was the Galleria that Hines copied it in Dallas, where Obata designed yet another luxury mall with a skating rink. It opened in 1982 and also included a Westin Hotel and multiple office towers.

In 1999, while prices for retail projects were strong, Hines sold the Houston Galleria to Urban Retail Properties; the deal included the office towers, hotels, and some adjoining raw land. Soon after, it sold the Dallas Galleria as well. Since then, the Houston Galleria has changed hands yet again. It's now owned by Simon Property Group, which controls nearly a third of America's large malls and can cut multiple-location deals for chain retailers.

The Galleria remains, by a mile, the most popular mall in Texas, drawing nearly twenty-four million visitors a year. At 2.4 million square feet, it is the fifth-largest mall in the U.S., generally listed as Houston's top tourist attraction. The Galleria's Neiman Marcus remains one of the chain's most profitable stores. But perhaps more astounding than the growth of the Galleria is the growth of the area around it, which has, more or less, become a new downtown, bigger than downtown Amsterdam or Cologne. Uptown Houston, as the area is officially designated, is now the biggest mixed-use development outside a downtown anywhere, with 14 percent of Houston's total office space—much of it developed by Hines. Uptown has far more retail and high-rise apartments than Houston's downtown. There are twenty-six hotels, roughly one hundred restaurants, and two thousand companies. Hines' headquarters are now located in the sixty-four-story Williams Tower, a Hines project designed by Johnson/Burgee that is connected to the Galleria via a skywalk.

In 1992, *Washington Post* writer Joel Garreau wrote the book *Edge City*, in which he noted that much of the United States' growth was in quasi-downtowns like the Galleria area. He opened one chapter by describing the astonishing, complicated variety of human activity he saw from the window of his hotel atop the mall.

John Breeding, president of the Uptown Houston District, says that although the office market became saturated during the half decade following the turn of the millennium, housing development—mainly luxury high-rise lofts and mid-rise condos—experienced a remarkable increase. "It's like Renaissance Italy," he says. "The piazza is built around the market. The Galleria has become the center of the city, and people want to live in the center of the city."

With that residential development, Uptown has become fully mixed-use, combining office, retail, and residential space. Gerald Hines' vision—that the Galleria would be a new downtown—now seems almost modest. In many ways, the development it spawned has become more urban than Houston's actual downtown.

The Houston Galleria and the sixty-four-story Williams Tower, a Hines project designed by Johnson/Burgee that is connected to the Galleria via a skywalk. The Galleria stimulated the growth of the surrounding area, resulting in Uptown Houston, now the largest mixed-use development outside a downtown anywhere. It contains 14 percent of Houston's total office space—much of it developed by Hines. Uptown has far more retail and high-rise apartments than Houston's downtown. There are twenty-six hotels, roughly one hundred restaurants, and two thousand companies. Hines is headquartered in the Williams Tower.

4

1983:
Wells Fargo Center
Denver

1987   1988   1989   1990   1991

1981:
Three First National Plaza
Chicago

1982:
101 California
San Francisco

1991:
Comerica Tower at Detroit Center
Detroit

MAKING A
MARK

MARK ON THE NATION

2002:
745 Seventh Avenue
New York City

1999   2000   2001   2002

2007:
300 North LaSalle
Chicago

2005   2006   2007

Making a Mark on the Nation
by Hilary Lewis

Hines now operates worldwide, but its roots lie firmly in Texas, where the company first made its mark. The early years were spent focusing on Houston at a time when that city was just beginning its explosive twentieth-century growth. By the 1970s, other nearby cities such as Austin, Midland, and New Orleans became part of the Hines orbit. This was possible due to Hines' business approach, which utilizes equity partners who share the risks and rewards of development. That strategy placed Hines on the same team with financial institutions, some of whom had operations outside of Houston, which opened critical doors to development opportunities in other cities in Texas and beyond. Once that leap was made–from being a purely local developer to one that could take its skills on the road–Hines had set the tone of its business model for decades to come. ▦ Jeffrey C. Hines, president of Hines and the son of founder and chairman Gerald D. Hines, describes the firm's business strategy: "Dad and our first CFO, Perry Waughtal, went a completely different direction from everyone else in real estate and embraced a structure in which, for each project, we would have one institutional investor who would bring substantially all of the capital for the project–all equity, no debt. Clearly, when you do that you have to give up a much larger slice of ownership. But you are left with a smaller piece of a much larger and safer pie, as opposed to a larger share of a smaller and much riskier pie. If you are going to be in business for the long term, that is a good way to go. There are ups and downs in real estate. Leverage is great on the upside, but it will kill you on the downside."

The move into other cities is remarkable for a development firm. Most development requires such specific local knowledge that many firms resist working in wide geographic areas. Hines was able to accomplish this not by ignoring the specifics of local conditions, but by immersing itself in those conditions and establishing multiple regional offices, all of which are essentially development firms themselves—but have the advantage of being closely linked with the expertise and experience of the Houston headquarters. Gerald Hines describes this organization: "Hines is really made up of many groups of development teams. There is a group in New York, a group in San Francisco, one in Chicago, and so on. . . . They are all separate small groups that are supported by central staff and discipline. But the ideas—the entrepreneurship—stem from those small groups."

Hines' foray into high-rise buildings outside Houston came in 1972 with One Shell Square in New Orleans, a Skidmore, Owings & Merrill project that followed on the heels of One Shell Plaza that Hines and the firm did in Houston. The following year the company formed Hines Banking Group to target commercial banks as users and joint venture partners. Buildings created during this initiative were located throughout the country, including Springfield, Illinois; Cincinnati, Ohio; Charleston, West Virginia; Minneapolis, Minnesota; and Spokane and Seattle, Washington.

This expansion into other markets occurred at a particularly interesting time in architecture, when many architects began to explore new approaches to formal geometry, diverse materials, and a variety of methods that differed greatly from the modernist model that had been so accepted for corporate architecture. Hines had done precisely this in Houston, to widespread acclaim, when it built

Pennzoil Place in 1975, a two-tower complex designed by Philip Johnson and John Burgee. This design created a striking silhouette on the Houston skyline based on Johnson/Burgee's sharp-edged tops—the result, Johnson described, of his becoming "bored with the box." When it came time to build RepublicBank Center—completed in 1983 and now Bank of America Center—just across the street, Johnson and Burgee developed an entirely different artistic direction. However, Johnson would credit Gerald Hines for inspiration: "Right away, Gerry conceived a better approach. He told me something that has stayed with me ever since: what was needed for this new building, he explained, was the 'point of difference.'"

Gerald Hines' first contribution to the Houston skyline, left, was an impressive one. One Shell Plaza (the white rectangular building with the prominent antenna) was the largest building in Texas at the time it was built. Hines went on to erect several other buildings that would define downtown Houston, including the Bank of America Center, right.

Hines' influence on the Houston skyline is evidenced by the array of standout buildings: From left, the tan stone and glass 717 Texas; the tall, slim JPMorgan Chase Tower; the twin black trapezoids of Pennzoil Place; the red granite neo-Gothic Bank of America Center; the sleek, antenna-clad One Shell Plaza; and 1100 Louisiana, with its rose granite façade and series of stepped bays at its crown.

While Hines moved into other markets for specific projects, it was not until 1979 that the firm opened a regional office. The first was the West, based in San Francisco, which would oversee local projects such as 580 California in 1984. This office would work in Northern California but go on to do prominent work in Los Angeles and beyond.

In 1981, the East regional office would open in New York; projects such as 53rd At Third in Manhattan were produced by that team, along with work throughout the Northeast. The Southeast office opened in 1982 in Atlanta, and would oversee projects from Atlanta to Miami. An example of its work was Miami's Wachovia Financial Center in 1984.

Hines would open one more U.S. regional office in 1986, one that would cover the Midwest from its base in Chicago. This would not mark the end of Hines' expansion. That would be continued internationally, beginning in Berlin in 1991 and later followed by additional offices in Europe, Asia, and Latin America. By 1986, however, Hines had established the structure of its U.S. operations, which would greatly enhance the firm's ability to provide services throughout the United States.

At left, the award-winning Wachovia Financial Center stands fifty-five stories on South Biscayne Boulevard in downtown Miami. Designed by Skidmore, Owings & Merrill, it is the tallest commercial office high-rise in Florida, offering breathtaking views of the Atlantic Ocean and the cityscape. The *Wall Street Journal* named it one of the nation's fifty best buildings in 1997.

Overall, the regional offices operate primarily in their named areas. Similar to an airport hub system, each office is based in a major city with easy access to multiple markets nearby. The leadership of each regional office has the expertise—and relationships—to make projects come to fruition, both within its own city and also in neighboring states.

As Hines expanded across the nation, it maintained the formula for spectacular buildings that it had developed in Houston: working with top architects to create what would become the signature towers of their respective cities. Philip Johnson and John Burgee would go on to produce numerous buildings for Hines, all distinctive structures that would stand out in any marketplace. But Johnson and Burgee were hardly the only architects selected by Hines for this expansion program. In fact, a significant number of internationally acclaimed architectural firms including Skidmore, Owings & Merrill, I. M. Pei & Partners (now Pei Cobb Freed & Partners), Robert A. M. Stern Architects, and Cesar Pelli & Associates (now Pelli Clarke Pelli Architects) all found significant work with Hines.

Johnson was one of the leading supporters of the architectural trend that reincorporated historic forms into architecture, what would be popularly known as postmodernism. He was therefore particularly adept at creating designs that read as icons. Johnson was not only interested in symbolism and architecture, from reintroducing Dutch gables to bringing back the glory of stone-clad buildings to American skyscrapers, but he was also committed to architectural quality, both in design and materials. Gerald Hines didn't need much convincing

One Ninety One Peachtree in Atlanta, designed by Philip Johnson and John Burgee, is a fifty-story skyscraper clad in granite, right. The structure appears to be two towers, since the central portion is recessed (allowing for more corner offices). It is capped by two graceful columned tops, giving the building a distinct skyline identity. It has won the prestigious Building Owners and Managers Association award three times.

that quality was king in the buildings he produced. But certainly, Johnson's approach resonated with him. Noted architect Cesar Pelli suggests, "Philip Johnson was more influential on Hines than anyone else. His ideas on architecture reached Gerald Hines first." When it came time for Hines to export its values to a broader audience, the firm gave multiple opportunities to Johnson and Burgee, who were never shy about using marble, granite, monumental proportions, and a commitment to new explorations in design.

Johnson's work with Hines produced an incredible portfolio of distinctive structures, which were overwhelmingly well received in their respective markets. In San Francisco, Johnson and Burgee produced two buildings on the same street that could not have been more different in design: 101 California (1982) with its sleek, modern geometry and 580 California (1984) with a mansard roof, replete with ornamental statues. In New York, the architects produced 53rd At Third (1986), remarkable for its oval plan, which Johnson suggested came from his love of the baroque period, but was also due to important input from Gerald Hines: "Normally when an architect suggests

Located in the heart of San Francisco's financial district, 101 California is a forty-eight-story tower encompassing 1.2 million square feet of office space. The sleek, modern tower is cylindrical in shape with articulated edges of alternating bands of granite and glass. It features a seven-story, glass-enclosed lobby at its base. Designed by Philip Johnson and John Burgee, 101 California was completed in 1982.

The fifty-two-story Figueroa at Wilshire in Los Angeles, completed in 1990, is clad in Brazilian Rose polished granite, accented with bronze panels, and complemented by gray glazed windows. The distinctive lobby incorporates two seventy-five-feet high atria with granite walls and floors, custom bronze chandeliers, and award-winning tropical landscaping. The property features an open-air plaza distinguished by a thirty-six-foot tall sculpture showcasing two bronze columns that combine water and fire. Hines sold the property in 2005.

something out of the ordinary, which usually means something more expensive, the client resists. Not Hines. That striking silhouette at 53rd At Third made that building," commented Johnson on the structure now commonly known among New Yorkers as the "Lipstick Building."

From the Hines-Johnson partnership, Atlanta would get a twin-peaked building at One Ninety One Peachtree, reminiscent of 1920s New York. Denver's Wells Fargo Center (completed in 1983 as the United Bank Center) was a study in juxtaposed solids that even Johnson admitted seemed to indicate the form of a cash register, but was intended to be a reference to arches, while Washington, D.C.'s Franklin Square (1989) remains an elegant reinterpretation of the district's tradition of classical architecture and its horizontality. Comerica Tower at Detroit Center (1991) has Gothic and Flemish qualities that reinforce the building's verticality. Each building had its own imagery and style, but all had a certain consistency in terms of materials and proportions. This came not only from Johnson and Burgee but also from the collaboration with Hines.

Cesar Pelli began working with Hines on Norwest Center (now Wells Fargo Center) in Minneapolis (1987), one of that city's most noted landmarks. Pelli's firm would eventually build a series of striking buildings for Hines, including the Owens Corning World Headquarters (1996) in Toledo, Ohio; the Enron Tower (2002, now 1500 Louisiana) in Houston; the JPMorgan Chase Building (2002) in San Francisco; and a striking tower proposed for the airspace above South Station in Boston. Pelli states the importance of Hines succinctly: "Hines became the biggest client we have ever had."

An interesting thing happened when Hines brought its talents to Boston with Five Hundred Boylston, another design from Johnson and Burgee. A dramatic, white tower with refined classical elements and an expansive courtyard more typical of the monumental work of Charles McKim in New York than of the more reserved, brick-clad structures often found in Boston, Five Hundred Boylston generated mixed reactions from its conservative Massachusetts audience. Although Hines had planned to build another structure alongside Five Hundred Boylston from Johnson and Burgee, the firm changed course in response to public opinion and elected to bring in another well-known figure in the world of architecture, Robert A. M. Stern, renowned for his commitment to preservation and keen understanding of historic architecture.

Stern's response was to return to the material Bostonians most associate with their beloved city: brick. At Two Twenty Two Berkeley, he was given an opportunity to contrast the existing Johnson/Burgee work with an adjacent skyscraper. Although Stern's firm was best known for residential and institutional work, Gerald Hines had no reservations about using Stern for such a task. Hines, always farsighted, was also extremely competent in managing architects.

Stern recalls what made working with Gerald Hines so successful: "Gerry gets the big picture very quickly, and he has a very good eye for detail. Actually, he has a frightening eye for detail—he can take one look at something and say, 'Bob, change that.' Actually, that's a very good thing when I am showing him a design. Gerry understands the little things that make the

Above, the glass façade of 191 North Wacker in Chicago (right) makes the most of its riverfront setting, complementing the waters of the Chicago River. Designed by Kohn Pedersen Fox, the thirty-seven-story office tower is located in the thriving West Loop submarket of Chicago's central business district. In 2006, Hines acquired its neighbor, 333 West Wacker (left). The Wells Fargo Center in Minneapolis, opposite, was the first project that Hines and Cesar Pelli undertook together. After it was completed in 1987, it became one of the city's most noted landmarks.

Hines entered the Denver real estate market in 1983 with the development of the fifty-two-story Wells Fargo Center. Designed by Philip Johnson and John Burgee, the skyscraper features attractive granite and gray glass exterior walls, and a breathtaking, glass-enclosed pavilion that soars over one hundred feet.

2001   2002   2003

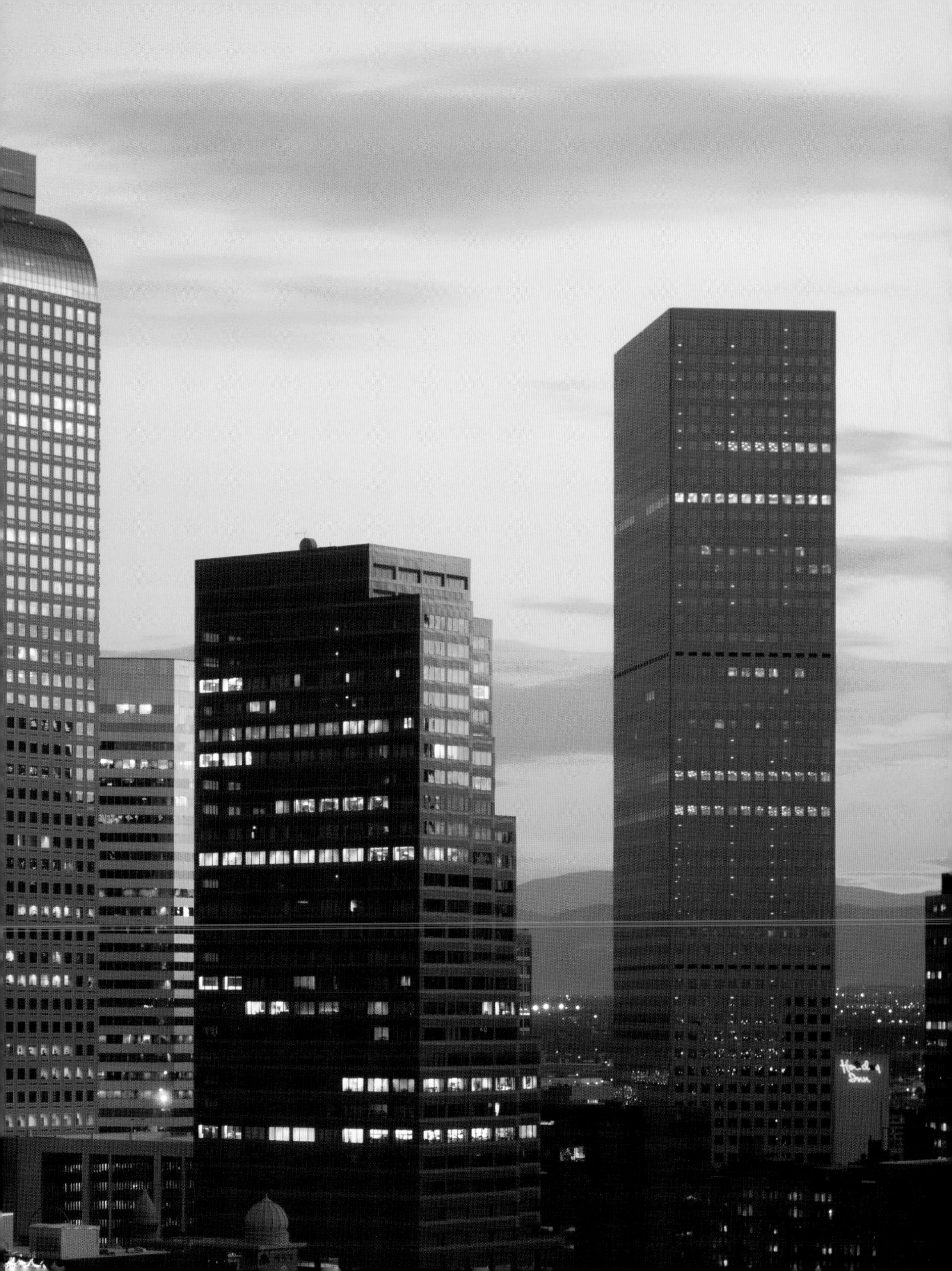

Above, One Shell Square, at the time the tallest building in Louisiana. The Skidmore, Owings & Merrill–designed tower was the first high-rise on Poydras Street. After that, Poydras became the main street in New Orleans.

lobby special." From Boston to Barcelona to Aspen, Hines would continue to work with Robert A. M. Stern Architects, creating distinctive properties that work contextually in their many settings.

Another one of the great architectural firms that have become part of the Hines portfolio is Skidmore, Owings & Merrill. The firm was one of the earliest architectural partners in the history of Hines, first working in Houston and then participating in the early expansion into other cities with One Shell Square (1972) in New Orleans. That fifty-story tower was the tallest structure in the state when it was built. Nearly identical to One Shell Plaza (1971) in Houston, the tower is a pure modern statement clad in travertine located on Poydras, today the heart of the New Orleans business district.

One Shell Square was an audacious project for New Orleans, a conservative city suspicious of outsiders—especially ones from Texas, says retired executive Louis Sklar. Gerald Hines hired longtime New Orleans resident Joe Ranna as the project officer to shepherd the complicated deal. "Joe knew how to get things done in New Orleans and was more patient on those matters than Gerry," says Sklar.

Ranna recalls that the biggest hurdle with One Shell Square was getting it leased. He cobbled together a whopping seventy-five leases to fill out the space's fifty floors. "The project was somewhat overbuilt, but it was a top-notch building and we got it leased—eventually."

Gerald Hines notes that this was the first office building on the street. "It was an outstanding building, and all of a sudden Poydras Street became the primary business address in New Orleans."

For Hines, building better buildings is a smart business decision. He states, "Architecture can lead not just to more profit, but to the mitigation of risk." He explains, "If you design something in a B location, and you put an outstanding piece of architecture there, the chances of pulling it off are much better."

This approach impressed not only clients and financial partners, but also other developers. Joey Kaempfer of the Kaempfer Company of Washington, D.C., recalls his initial reaction to Hines' work: "Gerry had produced a building in Washington that simply took my breath away—Columbia Square designed by Harry Cobb of Pei Cobb Freed in 1987."

Kaempfer applauds the accomplishments of Hines and the firm's ability to continually produce high-quality architecture. "Early on I learned a lesson from Gerry—it doesn't cost anything extra to design a building well, not really," states Kaempfer. "In the end, everyone—the developer, tenants, all users—benefit from a better building, a better product."

In the 1980s and 1990s, Skidmore, Owings & Merrill would continue to produce high-quality designs for Hines' corporate clients. From the PNC Center (1979) and Chemed Center at 255 Fifth (1991) in Cincinnati to Three First National Plaza (1981) in Chicago, and the Huntington Center (1984) in Columbus, Ohio, the firm designed buildings that had a distinct presence on the skyline of each city. The Wachovia Financial Center (1984) in Miami is one of that city's signature waterfront buildings.

The move into the Midwest, in particular into Cincinnati, Columbus, Chicago, and Louisville, was overseen by a number of principals formerly based in Houston. Michael Topham would eventually set up a full Midwest office, today run by executive vice president Kevin Shannahan. Shannahan recalls the firm's increasing activity in the 1980s and 1990s in the Midwest. "In Cleveland, we were received with open arms because we were not perceived as outsiders. We built local relationships and established a reputation with key partners. These were critical factors for our success." Hines would produce multiple buildings in Cleveland, but Shannahan points out the importance of the Huntington Center (1984). As opposed to new development, this project was a renovation of a 1920s classical structure, which created a lot of goodwill in the community.

Now that Jeffrey Hines has taken on the role of president, says David Childs of Skidmore, Owings & Merrill, the transition from father to son is impressive. "Jeff Hines is a very strong leader and quite different in his approach from Gerry Hines. That sort of succession is so unusual. It is a testament to Gerry Hines' style of leadership that this is possible." If Gerald Hines had been more of a typical developer, or "swashbuckler," as Childs describes it, it would have been difficult for such a strong successor to emerge from within the system. Childs is emphatic: "The firm is an outgrowth of Gerald Hines' personality, but it continues to grow under his son's leadership. What an achievement to be able to pass along such an organization to an extraordinary man like Jeff."

Commenting on how the firm is moving increasingly into the international arena, Jeff Hines says: "What we are trying to do is

Huntington Center in Columbus, Ohio, is a thirty-seven-story office tower containing one million square feet. Completed in 1984, the building is clad in imperial red granite and bronze-tone glass. The office tower features four atriums, one at street level and one each on levels thirteen, twenty, and twenty-eight. Designed by Skidmore, Owings & Merrill, the development incorporates 27,000 square feet of retail space, a one-thousand-car parking facility, and a 30,000-square-foot athletic club.

5   2006   2007

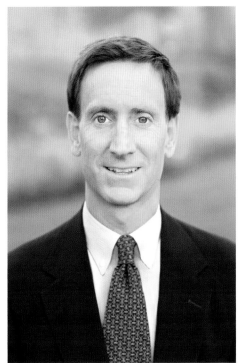

the same thing that Dad and the rest of the firm were able to do in the mid-1970s when Hines branched out from Houston. Then, as now, we need to try and combine becoming a local player with being a larger operation. This takes a while, either to learn or hire the right local knowledge for the marketplace and marry that with what we, as a larger firm, can bring to the table."

For decades, Hines has produced skyline-defining buildings, from Houston to San Francisco and New York to Atlanta. These very buildings have frequently become landmarks—often shaping the image of those cities. Along with the firm's professional acumen and the wise decision to establish its professionals in key cities throughout the country, it is the product itself—the buildings—that has distinguished Hines nationwide and made it possible for the firm

to succeed in so many markets and expand internationally. Often willing to try something out of the ordinary, but always with an eye toward fine workmanship, materials, and details, Hines exported to the rest of the country what it had begun in Houston in the 1950s—the elevation of commercial building to the realm of fine architecture.

"Hines operates in so many different markets they cannot possibly build the same sorts of buildings in all cities," A. Eugene Kohn, chairman of Kohn Pedersen Fox Associates, once said. "Instead, they are simply the best in any given market. That's something—they have consistency across the world. Amazing."

Hines continues to grow under Jeff Hines, above right, who has been president since 1990. Hines worked his way up the ranks in the firm, offering a strong financial orientation to complement his father's visionary, project-oriented approach. The firm is building a sustainable national organization by combining the strength of its central office with local expertise. Kevin Shannahan, above left, brings that regional expertise to his role as the officer responsible for the development and asset management of projects in the Midwest and Southeast regions of the U.S. and in South America.

GROWING A

A panorama of Diagonal Mar in Barcelona, right. Hines took over a long-troubled shopping center site bordering the Mediterranean and turned it into one of the highest-profile lifestyle centers in Europe. In taking on the site for the Diagonal Mar shopping center, Hines was also given responsibility for the master planning of a much larger site that included a new park and sophisticated high-rise housing. Far right, the lobby of EDF Tower in Paris.

RGANIZATION

Growing a Global Organization
by Laura Rowley

In 1989, the world was transformed in ways no one could have predicted. Tens of thousands of Chinese students took over Beijing's Tiananmen Square in April to rally for democracy. A month later, Mikhail Gorbachev, whose program of glasnost opened the door to new political, economic, and social freedoms across the communist world, became president of the Soviet Union. The Berlin Wall, a symbol of rancor between the Soviets and the West for twenty-eight years, was demolished by euphoric crowds that autumn. More than forty-two years of communist rule ended in the Czech Republic as Václav Havel, a well-known playwright and dissident, was elected president. Watching these momentous developments from their offices around the U.S., the leaders of Hines saw irresistible opportunity. Although the company had worked on projects in Canada, Mexico, and even the Middle East as early as the 1970s, the historic events of 1989 would propel Hines to its destiny as a global player. ▧

By 2006, Hines would have operations in sixteen countries and an international portfolio spanning the real estate spectrum. A sampling: the largest mixed-use developments in Spain, France, and Italy; major mixed-use complexes in Berlin; 145 homes in Prague; office buildings in Paris and Rio de Janeiro; residential, office, industrial, and distribution centers in Mexico; high-rise condominiums in Beijing; a luxury residential community in Moscow. Hines would also establish itself in international asset management, leasing, and advisory services.

A FOUNDER'S WANDERLUST

Although 1989 would mark a turning point, company founder Gerald Hines never shied away from far-flung real estate opportunities. "Gerry was always very curious and interested in the foreign markets, because most of them had no competition whatsoever for the quality that we did," says retired executive vice president Louis Sklar. He adds with a chuckle: "On the flip side, most of them had no demand for the quality we did."

At least one international firm did seek out Hines' quality in the 1970s—Louis Dreyfus Property Group, a subsidiary of the 155-year-old conglomerate based in Paris. The firm entered into a joint venture with Hines to build a ten-story office tower called Les Terrasses in Montreal, Canada, which was completed in 1976.

Hines made its second international foray south of the U.S. border as the result of a chance meeting. In 1968, Gerald Hines and his family attended the summer Olympics in Mexico. His guide was a young Mexican named Alfredo "Tito" Elias Jr., who went on to graduate from engineering

school and receive an MBA from Harvard in 1975. Elias proposed a joint venture with Hines shortly after graduating. "We formed a development with Hines as the 49-percent partner, because under Mexican law, a citizen had to have a majority interest in the company," says Sklar. In 1977, they completed their first project: Condominio Homero y Racine, a twenty-four-unit, 100,000-square-foot condominium in Mexico City.

The Mexican economy declined sharply in the 1980s, halting Hines' activities. But the firm would revive its interest a decade later with the development of Del Bosque, a 795,000-square-foot complex in Mexico City designed by Cesar Pelli. In 1992, Hines opened its office in the capital and began construction on Del Bosque's two condominium towers and thirteen-story office building, which the Coca-Cola Company later purchased for its Latin American headquarters. Hines would greatly expand its presence in Mexico in the years to come, executing award-winning new developments of office, industrial, and residential properties as well as acquisitions and renovations.

Hines dipped its toe in the waters of the Middle East in the mid-1970s. Michael Topham, executive vice president of Europe and the Middle East, joined Hines in 1975, having previously worked in Kuwait. "Gerry said to me, 'You know your way around the Middle East—go see if you can build a business there,'" Topham recalls. He launched fledgling operations in Greece, Iran, and Egypt, where the company broke ground on a mixed-used project for the Arab International Bank in Cairo in 1977. "We had excavated and driven pilings, but we never finished it—one of the Mideast wars stopped the funding," recalls Topham. "And if it weren't for the fact that the Shah of Iran became persona non grata, we'd still be building; our person took the last flight out of Tehran before the shah fell."

Hines also made an early entry into China. As Sklar recalls, "Gerry walked into my office and said, 'We got a call from someone at Chase and there is this deal in China. I figure this is just crazy enough that we'd be interested.'" Chase Bank, Turner Construction International, and Kaiser Engineers had a deal with the

In 1992, Hines opened an office in Mexico City and began construction on Del Bosque, a thirteen-story office building with two condominium towers comprising 795,000 square feet. The Coca-Cola Company later purchased the Cesar Pelli–designed tower for its Latin American headquarters.

At the Hines Beijing
office (from left)
Yuki Cai, Lin Chao,
and David He. Hines
explored opportunities
in China as early as
1982, but decided the
timing was not right.
Its first development
was Embassy House,
a luxury apartment
development designed
for expatriates and
diplomats, completed
in 2002.

Chinese to build a foreign trade center. "We were doing preliminary soil samples, engineering, and design," says Sklar. "In 1982 or 1983, the Chinese realized that they had, through many ventures, contracted for far more than they could pay for and canceled the contract."

Hines investigated a second opportunity in China in the mid-1980s, but concluded the timing was premature. "The Chinese tended to be on all sides of the deal," Sklar explains. "You acquired land under some sort of lease agreement, the terms of which were dictated by the Chinese; the contractor was Chinese; the financing was guaranteed by Bank of China; and to put frosting on the cake, if you wanted to rent to IBM, the Chinese might have a building they wanted IBM to be in, and they wouldn't let them lease space from you. The economic opportunity was controlled by the Chinese partner, and we had all the risk. That was not a formula that appealed to us."

Then the Berlin Wall came tumbling down. Hines' global expansion officially began in the fall of 1989, during an executive committee meeting of the company's various business units. "We could not avoid seeing the dramatic geopolitical changes that permitted economic globalization—prospects that had never existed in our lifetimes," explains E. Staman Ogilvie, executive vice president for the Eurasia region, who joined Hines in 1973. "We recognized a set of demand factors that resembled the United States after World War II: obsolete building stock, huge potential economic growth, new entrants to the workforce, and very hungry, interested consumers."

At that meeting, Hines' five senior leaders, who all had full-time duties in the U.S., each agreed to tackle a region of the world: Ogilvie would go to Russia, the Czech Republic, Poland, and Hungary;

Topham, a British native, signed on for Western Europe; Sklar took Mexico and South America; James Buie, based on the West Coast, agreed to explore China and other parts of Asia; and Chip Davidson raised his hand for Scandinavia.

TOUGH TIMES IN TEXAS

But the dramatic shift in the global landscape was just one element that triggered international expansion. The other was the implosion of the commercial real estate market at home. Texas' petroleum-based economy skyrocketed in the early 1980s, as the Iran-Iraq war and other crises in the Middle East prompted a more than tenfold increase in the price of oil—from around $3 a barrel in 1973 to $37 by 1981. The oil industry—and the service companies and small businesses that served it—boomed, and banks made significant loans to help them increase production. Meanwhile, recent federal regulations had allowed commercial banks to make such loans for the first time and relaxed lending standards, and a new tax law encouraged passive investment in real estate. Awash in capital, developers raced to erect office buildings, apartments, retail space, and single-family homes.

And then it ended—badly. Oil prices plummeted to $11 a barrel. By 1985, more than 30 million square feet of office space stood vacant in Houston, and the city's unemployment rate hit 12.6 percent the following year. Statewide, 425 banks failed, and nine of the ten largest bank holding companies failed or had to be recapitalized in the 1980s. In 1989, 65 percent of total U.S. bank failures were in Texas, and less than one-quarter of Texas thrifts were both profitable and solvent, according to the Dallas Federal Reserve.

Jim Buie, executive vice president of Hines' Western U.S. and Asia Pacific regional office, joined Hines in 1980. Buie has supervised the firm's growing body of work in China.

Workers dig into another phase of Park Avenue, Hines' five-tower, 2.6-million-square-foot condominium located on the southern edge of Beijing's Chaoyang Park, the largest urban green space in China. The first tower was designed with 270 condominiums. Hines recognized substantial demand for larger apartments, so it built the second tower with 210 units, which sold out almost immediately.

"When the Houston market crashed, the rest of the country said, 'Houston's problem is that oil fell in price and the Mexican peso went through the floor—but we don't have that problem in . . . ' fill in the name of the city," says Sklar. "Many real estate developers failed to see the oversupply. We saw a six-year supply of office space coming on the market." So Hines did something it had never done since its founding in 1957: it sold some of its buildings, providing enough cash to shore up the company in Houston.

With no development on the horizon for years, Hines switched strategy. It partnered with General Motors' pension fund to buy existing properties for the first time. "When the development business in the U.S. fell apart, we knew that we were going to start to buy buildings other people had developed, which was something we had never done," says C. Hastings "Hasty" Johnson, executive vice president and chief financial officer, who joined Hines in 1978. "We did a series of $100 million partnerships with GM, working together to buy buildings. That was the first time we arranged capital in advance of what we thought would happen in the market." The GM venture marked the beginning of a transition from financing one-off deals to creating investment pools with specific strategies— a concept that would prove crucial to Hines' success in emerging markets.

Meanwhile, Hines knew that if the company wanted to keep the best people and provide growth opportunities, it would have to go abroad. "We basically had a development firm with no development to do," says Johnson. "If you foresee no development for eight years, you either turn into a property management firm only, or you expand internationally."

International growth would evolve organically, with Hines opening offices

in response to specific opportunities. That meant the expansion would play out differently in each market. But one aspect of the strategy was universal: Hines moved carefully, investing the time and money to build a long-term sustainable organization that was managed locally but steeped in the firm's culture.

Neil Jones, senior vice president, worked with Ogilvie to open operations in Russia, then moved to London to assist with Western Europe. "There was no pretense that someone like me could come in and say, 'This is the way we do it back in Texas,'" says Jones. "That wouldn't work in New York, much less Paris. It was a very gradual, methodical effort to find the right people."

"Real estate is a local business," adds Topham. "Relationships in development, government, banking, property, and advertising are very important. The success of Hines without any question has been to build local teams. Although for some period

Above, executive vice president for the Eurasia region E. Staman Ogilvie (right) with Eugene Ustinov of UpDK (left) and Michael Barash at the tenth anniversary of Hines' joint venture with UpDK. Ogilvie helped launch the company's operations in Russia, where Hines brought Western-style management to serve multinational clients before moving into development.

of time, we would send in a seasoned Hines executive to instill culture, values, risk underwriting, and know-how so the vision could be conveyed in the right way, and the Hines standards maintained internationally."

PROPERTY MANAGEMENT

In emerging markets, Hines initially brought Western-style management to serve multinational clients. Its first assignment in Russia, for example, was consulting and property management. "We thought it would not be prudent in 1990 to take the big equity risks of new development deals," says Jones. "We established a service company to get to understand the market before we could take big risks." Hines went into Moscow with a helping hand: an independent Dallas-area real estate entrepreneur and former Russian concert violinist named Michael Barash, who had arrived in the U.S. in 1979 with $12 in his pocket, introduced Hines to a Russian government agency known by the acronym UpDK.

For decades, UpDK had provided real estate and services to the foreign diplomatic corps and multinationals doing business in Russia. As a result it had substantial real estate holdings. "They recognized that with glasnost, there was going to be a lot of question as to whether they should continue to exist," says Ogilvie. "They wanted to differentiate and prove there was a reason for them to continue to enjoy a favored place in the real estate economy, and serve Westerners in the free market."

In 1991, UpDK contracted with Hines to help complete Park Place Moscow, a mixed-use complex in southeastern Moscow with 330 residential units, office space, an indoor shopping area, and other high-end amenities. Although the construction was well underway, Hines

adjusted the design to make the project more attractive to Westerners, provided a sophisticated leasing program, and managed the property.

"It gave us the opportunity to get established, learn the market, earn some money, and wait for the right time to take the equity risk," says Jones. Park Place Moscow became a magnet for Western diplomats and executives, and Hines attracted a dozen other property management assignments. By 2006, it had three million square feet under management in Russia.

Jones says building the operation in the "the Wild, Wild East" was the toughest assignment he's faced. "In 1990, hotels, restaurants, decent offices, places to live—none of those things existed at the quality level you wanted. For someone in the real estate business, therein lies the opportunity," he says. "At the same time we struggled with the same problems as other companies: How do you create an office? How can you get a copy machine? Who do you call when it breaks down? We were staying in Russian hotels where the room

Hines first moved into Russia through property management. In 1991, a quasi-government agency, UpDK, contracted with Hines to help complete Park Place Moscow, above, a mixed-use complex in southeastern Moscow with 330 residential units, office space, an indoor shopping area, and other high-end amenities. Although the construction was well underway, Hines adjusted the design to make the project more attractive to Westerners, provided a sophisticated leasing program, and managed the property.

Distribution Park Louveira, above and above left, a built-to-suit warehouse and office development for Exel-Kraft in Louveira, Brazil. In 1999, Hines and Trust Company of the West formed their second emerging markets real estate fund, which financed projects in Brazil, China, Mexico, Poland, and some Western European markets for risk mitigation.

was so narrow it was barely wider than the width of a single bed. There was no proper taxi system; if you needed to get from one meeting to the next, you'd hitchhike, flagging down the random car driving by."

Within just a few years, Hines would be ready to develop new construction in emerging markets. But first it would have to find the capital.

EMERGING MARKETS FINANCE

As Hines established itself in Russia and other emerging markets, in the U.S. the firm continued to work side by side with institutional investors on both acquisitions and build-to-suit developments. In the early 1990s, Hines teamed with Dean Witter Realty (now a subsidiary of Morgan Stanley Dean Witter and Company) and Trust Company of the West (TCW), which had potential work in China. Both sides concluded they would have a better shot at persuading other institutions to co-invest in emerging markets if they could offer a diversified portfolio of real estate that mitigated some of the risk.

In 1996, Hines founded the $410 million Emerging Markets Real Estate Fund I (EMREF I) with TCW and Dean Witter Realty to manage the acquisition, development, operation, and disposition of high-quality real estate in emerging market countries. The fund provided financing

for projects in Russia, China, Mexico, and Poland. In 1999, Hines and TCW formed a second fund totaling $436 million, Emerging Markets Real Estate Fund II, with projects in Brazil, China, Mexico, and Russia.

Hines began the first fund at a time when investors were skeptical about giving control of money to a developer. "It was thought to be crazy—that if a developer had money they would develop whether the project was needed or not," recalls Hasty Johnson. Hines decided to appoint a fund manager to oversee the investment pool—someone whose interests were aligned with the performance of the fund.

"The manager acts as a fiduciary—he or she is paid on how well the fund performs, not on how well Hines does," Johnson explains. "The people who work for Hines are concerned with their regions and real estate; the fund managers are concerned about the fund and its investors."

"We worked awfully hard to assemble the first tranche of money," recalls Sklar. "The presence of this fund gave us enormous credibility in negotiating with people. Over and over, Mexicans and South Americans were accustomed to developers coming down and having the 'long luncheon' and pledging eternal friendship—and trying to sell services. But if you brought equity with you, there was something to talk about. It gave us the financial muscle to be credible."

Since the inception of its 1991 acquisition fund with GM, Hines has formed twenty-one investment pools with various strategies, raising $10.1 billion in equity, according to Chris Hughes, senior vice president of fund-raising. "Investors looked at emerging markets and said it's better to be in a fund format, where there is diversification," Hughes explains. "To have exposure to China, Russia, Brazil, and Mexico—any one of those is better as a blended bet." The company's programmatic

Torre Almirante, above, was one of the projects funded through Hines' Emerging Markets Real Estate Fund II. Completed in 2004, the thirty-six-story tower is located in downtown Rio de Janeiro's business district and houses a single tenant, Petrobras.

A resident of Pokrovsky Hills in Moscow walks her child to the adjacent Anglo-American school. The proximity of the Anglo-American school made Pokrovsky Hills the most attractive community in the city for expatriates with children; the property still has a waiting list for every unit.

investing attracted U.S. and European pension funds, and became a critical tool to compete with well-capitalized real estate investment trusts.

Meanwhile, the fund manager structure gives Hines an unprecedented level of discretion over how it invests the fund. Each fund has a mandate, and Hines consults with investors only when the projects fall outside the stated parameters of the fund.

EMREF I financed a wave of new projects. Hines leaders had expected the strongest demand to come from multinational corporations seeking quality office space. But in Asia, Russia, and Eastern Europe in the early 1990s, most were clamoring for housing. Companies hoping to expand to China and Russia were having great difficulty attracting senior executives and their families. In Beijing, Buie recalls, "they would come, they would look, and they would leave, because they didn't find the existing housing stock to be adequate." Ogilvie discovered the same trend in Moscow and Prague.

As a result, the initial investments by the emerging markets fund were upscale residential communities geared toward expatriates and diplomats. In Beijing, Hines built Embassy House, 174 luxury apartments in a thirty-two-story tower with a swimming pool, health spa, library, café/deli, and bar. "We so strongly wanted to create a landmark and flagship for Hines," says Buie. "We started with the notion that we could create a project that would be at home in San Francisco, New York, or any of the major cities around the world.

We wanted to offer similar amenities and space at Embassy House. We overshot the mark a little bit—the apartments are as good or better than some in other cities. The building is populated by the who's who of the business and political world in China."

Although the site was identified in 1996, it took three years to slash through the red tape before construction could begin in the fall of 1999. "Much of the rule book was still being written," says David Lawrence, a retired senior vice president for Hines. "At one point we were told we would need 176 separate approvals, all indicated by a red stamp on the document, before we could begin construction." Embassy House was completed in 2002.

In Moscow, Hines developed Pokrovsky Hills, a 260-unit gated townhouse community. As part of the deal, Hines donated a portion of the site to the Anglo-American school in Moscow, which had outgrown its facilities and was operating in multiple locations. The project was a juggling act, Ogilvie recalls. "We had to finalize control of the site; lure the school, which had to do a capital-raising campaign large enough to build their building; negotiate with several government authorities who had some rights to say what happened on that land; and agree to put in utilities for the community." He explains, "We had to keep all the pieces together before we moved ahead. It was a very difficult enterprise, but Pokrovsky Hills has been the single biggest winner of anything we have done in the fund."

The proximity of the Anglo-American school made Pokrovsky Hills the most attractive community in the city for expatriates with children; the property still has a waiting list for every unit. Ogilvie says

Hines' status as a private company gave it the staying power to see the project through, which took six years from concept to completion in 2002. "There's a reason we're the only big American player with a global footprint," Ogilvie says. "We have no quarterly pressure, we don't have to broadcast our strategy, and we're not holding hands with people and explaining over and over again what we do. We are very efficient in dealing with investors in the private sphere, and have the authority to act broadly on our own wits."

Hines applied the Moscow strategy to its housing development in the Czech Republic, where it opened its Prague office in 1993. Mala Sarka, a high-quality residential development consisting of 145 single-family homes on a twenty-eight-acre site in the village of Nebusice, was developed just minutes from Prague's city center. The International School of Prague, the city's English-speaking school, was constructed adjacent to the property. The first phase of ninety homes was completed in 1997, and the second phase in 1999.

The Prague development required some unique entitlements. "There were claims from people who owned the land prior to World War II, when the Nazis took the land," says Johnson. "Because there is no title insurance available, we had to research who owned the land prior to World War II and find the families and make settlement with them. We had forty families at the closing who all received checks—some of the families had no idea they had owned the land until we contacted them."

By the turn of the twentieth century, with a solid foothold in emerging markets, Hines began targeting China's domestic marketplace. Its second residential development in Beijing, called Park Avenue, is a five-tower, 2.6-million-square-foot condominium located on the southern edge of Chaoyang Park, the largest urban green space in China. Groundbreaking was held in 2003.

"Park Avenue could not have been conceived in the mid-1990s because the market wasn't there," says Buie. "But over the last six years, there has been a growing demand by upper middle class Chinese, who are very interested in an improved living

Pokrovsky Hills, below, a townhome development near the center of Moscow, was a strenuous juggling act for Hines executives. They had to finalize control of the site; lure the school, which had to do a large capital-raising campaign to build their building; negotiate with several government authorities who had jurisdiction over the land; and install utilities for the community. It took six years from concept to completion, but the project has been the most successful investment in the firm's first Emerging Markets Fund.

Following the successful leasing and management of Ducat Place II, above left, for Liggett Tobacco in Moscow, Hines formed a joint venture with Liggett to develop Ducat Place III, rendering above right. The Class A office building was completed in 2006.

environment." The first tower was designed with 270 condominiums, but Hines found substantial demand for larger apartments, so it built the second tower with 210 units. "They sold out almost immediately," Buie says. "We made sure buyers felt they got good value for their money. We did fully sprinklered buildings, even though that is not required by code. We felt life safety was important; people appreciated that and were willing to pay for it."

China's nascent mortgage industry was key to Park Avenue's success. "That has only occurred over the last several years," Buie explains. "The government put out some very good mortgage rules and regulations that let people put down 10 to 20 percent and finance the rest. That has been a huge factor in the success of these developments and a stabilizing element for Chinese society."

OFFICE AND MIXED-USE

With capital from its Emerging Markets Funds, Hines moved nimbly from residential work to office and mixed-use developments in emerging markets across the globe. In 2001, it acquired Millennium Tower (now Hyundai Motor Tower), a twenty-four-story, 600,000-square-foot Class A office building in Beijing for $95 million from Hyundai Engineering & Construction Company of Korea. The building—designed by the late Minoru Yamasaki, the Japanese-American architect who designed the Twin Towers of New York City's World Trade Center—had been completed the previous year and was just 25 percent leased. Hines repositioned the project and brought occupancy up to 95 percent, leasing space to Microsoft and other multinationals before selling it to a different arm of Hyundai.

In Russia, Hines began working on sites where Liggett Tobacco had bought property from the Russian cigarette maker Ducat. Two buildings were situated on prime in-town locations where property values were rising. "Liggett hired us to manage and lease Ducat Place II, and we learned more about a third-party management assignment with a Western-style owner," says Ogilvie. "We also used that relationship to move across the street with the same owner and form a joint venture to develop Ducat Place III from scratch." The Class A office building was completed in 2006.

In Poland, Hines brought a new standard of quality to the market with Metropolitan, a multiuse office building on historic Pilsudski Square, designed by the British architect Lord Norman Foster.

In 1998, Hines opened its South American regional office in São Paulo, Brazil, and the next year announced plans to develop Panamérica Park, a 435,000-square-foot office/high-tech service center, with Itaúsa Empreendimentos, the real estate investment arm of Itaúsa, Brazil's second largest private company. It was completed in 2003.

In 2000, Hines began development of Torre Almirante, a thirty-six-story, 442,233-square-foot office tower in downtown Rio de Janeiro. Designed by American architectural firm Robert A. M. Stern Architects, the tower offers 360-degree views of Rio's stunning natural geography, including Guanabara Bay, Sugar Loaf Mountain, coastal mountains, and the Atlantic Ocean. The tower also features continuously changing lighting displays that reflect the vibrant colors of Rio. Petrobras, the Brazilian national oil company, leased the entire space in 2004. By 2006, Hines had a half

dozen industrial and distribution centers either completed or underway in Brazil.

In 2006, Hines began work on 21st Century Tower, the headquarters of financial institution China Everbright Group—and its largest venture in China. "They had a site in the Pudong financial district in Shanghai," says Buie. "They began excavation and laid a foundation, and then stopped it in the late '90s because they didn't feel they were on the right path. We convinced them that a mix of uses with an office at the bottom and hotel and residences at the top would meet the market demand." The fifty-story, mixed-use tower includes headquarters space for China Everbright; additional speculative Class A office space; a luxury 187-room Four Seasons Hotel; and, on the uppermost floors, fifty-two Four Seasons residences that will be among the most luxurious for-sale apartments in Shanghai.

Jeff Hines giving a speech in São Paulo, Brazil, in 1999, a year after the firm opened its South American regional office there. Hines subsequently built the landmark Torre Almirante office tower as well as other office parks and industrial and distribution centers in Brazil.

Hines opened its first
European office in
Berlin in 1992. Here,
Katharina Banit, senior
financial controller,
works with the famed
Friedrichstraße just
outside her window.

Hines' properties in Berlin: At left, Pariser Platz 3 combines the headquarters of DZ Bank with a ten-story luxury condominium; its façade reflects the historic Brandenburg Gate. Above, Hofgarten am Gendarmenmarkt offers a five-star hotel, shopping, and residential housing.

A LEARNING CURVE

While the demand in emerging markets started on the residential side, in developed countries such as Germany, France, Italy, Spain, and the United Kingdom, the need was for office and mixed-use properties. Tackling historic locations and massive, complex projects across Europe, Hines would build its brand on architectural excellence and quality construction.

In 1991, Hines opened its first European office, in Berlin. The branch started work on two projects simultaneously. The first was Hofgarten am Gendarmenmarkt, a mini Galleria of sorts, offering a five-star hotel, shopping, and residential housing. The second, Rosmarin Karree, was a mixed-use project with office space and 50,000 square feet of residential housing located in the heart of old Berlin. In both cases, Hines designed projects that fit aesthetically with Berlin's venerable eighteenth- and nineteenth-century architecture.

Hines' third project, Pariser Platz 3, was situated on one of the city's most historic sites—the great square at the Brandenburg Gate. In terms of prestige, it was like building across the street from the Washington Monument. Hines chose renowned architect Frank Gehry to design the project, which combines the headquarters of DZ Bank with a ten-story luxury condominium. The company moved on to major projects in Frankfurt, Düsseldorf, and Munich.

The European market provided plenty of learning curves, says Topham. "I always thought I knew everything about building office buildings, because we always built the most beautiful, award-winning buildings in the U.S. But Europeans don't want big, tall office buildings," he explains. "They want Washington, D.C.–scale cities. European cities are not Houston or Minneapolis—they are twenty-four-hour cities. So the projects must be mixed-use; you have to include shopping, residential, and other things that in America you don't."

Cultural and zoning issues also proved challenging in Europe. For example, the typical floorplate of a U.S. office building is about 25,000 square feet, and the distance from the elevator core wall to the windows is around forty feet, because that's the most efficient layout for offices, secretarial stations, and conference rooms, according to Jones. "Internationally, you throw all those things out the window," he says. "By law, German employees have a right to natural light. So there is no such thing as interior offices, and the typical floorplate must be substantially smaller." Meanwhile, ceiling heights must be more than ten feet, while nine feet is typical in the U.S.

Hines also had to design operable windows. "Even in a fifty-story office building the windows have to open, because culturally Germans want fresh air, even in the winter," Jones explains. "That's something we'd never do in the U.S., because open windows would mess up the air balancing systems and the air conditioning, and cause energy costs to go up. Germans think Americans work in suffocating boxes."

Even minor details commanded Hines' attention: beds in German hotel rooms, for instance, are 6'9" instead of the 6'1" typical in the U.S. "Our German staff said, 'If you don't put in 6'9" beds, you won't rent,'" Topham recalls. "We needed that local know-how, because we're creating something that can't be changed. Starbucks can change the taste of the coffee if they get it wrong—but if you get it wrong when you build a building, it sits there because it's steel and concrete. Going overseas is a thrilling experience, but it's humbling because there's so much that you don't know, which is compounded by foreign language."

The company met those humbling challenges by finding young, bright entrepreneurial locals and molding them according to the Hines philosophy. "There are five characteristics that speak to our culture: integrity, intelligence, initiative, interpersonal skills, and perseverance," Jones explains. "That goes back to the founder and his son Jeff Hines, who exhibit that behavior and philosophy. They are entrepreneurial, but not people who seek the limelight. Our focus is on the quality of

the building, the management, the design— and we let that speak for itself."

Hines executives met with brokers, city officials, opinion leaders, and business leaders to learn about each market. "But our hidden agenda was to find people," says Hines senior vice president Jay Wyper. "We get to know and like people and a year or two later they are on board. We were in no rush, because once you find the right people, you can do anything." Once hired, new Hines executives come to the U.S. for training and to network with people around the globe in the same position, who become internal resources.

Hines also structures its compensation so that executives have a financial stake in a project's success. "When they make decisions, they are making decisions as a partner—they win or lose if that project wins or loses," says Topham. "They have that real sense of ownership, which goes into the concept of integrity. You feel like

a partner. You are only going to make a recommendation if it makes sense for yourself and the Hines family."

In the 1990s, Hines opened offices in Western Europe in quick succession: Paris, Frankfurt, and the European regional office in London in 1995; Barcelona in 1996; and Milan in 1999. In some cases, Hines started offices from scratch; in others, it acquired existing firms.

Karl Franz Wambach, managing director of Hines' German operations, joined the firm in 1993. A civil engineer by training, Wambach had managed numerous projects in Germany and the Middle East for general contractors, supervising projects valued at up to $1 billion.

"I was overwhelmed by the personal touch of Gerald D. Hines and also by Michael Topham, who were not only interested in my career, but also in my life and my family," Wambach recalls. He says he was attracted to the company's flat management structure, and the

Hines project manager Christopher Reschke, in the marketing center of a new development in Berlin. Hines has built its international operations by carefully cultivating local talent who understand their market and can better spot potential opportunities. They also offer the cultural insight, knowledge of governmental regulations, and networks of contacts crucial to a project's success.

ability to bring new ideas directly to top management: "Mr. Hines and all his senior staff listen seriously to the opinions of their partners." Wambach says Hines has succeeded in Germany where other foreigners have failed because the company connects its global knowledge base to local leadership, which understands the market and business networks.

In Milan, for example, Hines found a ten-person, family-owned firm to set up Hines Italia. "If we go in and spend the time to understand the dynamics of the market, well, even a blind pig finds a truffle every now and then," says Wyper. "But if you dig with local people who understand the market, you have a better chance of finding an opportunity to buy something on the cheap, or develop something to respond to a particular need."

With its partners, that's exactly what Hines identified in Milan: a fifty-six-acre piece of land that hadn't been developed for forty years. "We optioned most of the sites and were able to put together a unique public-private partnership," says Wyper. The municipality owned some of the land, and Hines created a master plan under which the provincial government would develop one part, the city another, and Hines a third. The massive urban planning project, called Porta Nuova, includes office and retail space, and a twenty-six-acre public park.

Milan provides an example of the massive, highly complicated, and expensive ventures that have become a Hines specialty. As Sklar explains: "We don't ever choose projects because they are complicated. But we like complicated projects because the barrier to entry is higher; there are far fewer players on the field when you have to invest a significant amount of capital— and personal capital—before you even know if you have a project."

A rendering of Porta Nuova in Milan, a fifty-six-acre development for which Hines created the master plan. The massive urban planning project involves a public-private partnership, and includes office, residential, and retail space, as well as a twenty-six-acre public park. The project exemplifies the large, complex ventures that have become a Hines specialty in international markets.

In 2004 Hines broke
ground on the 484,200-
square-foot Meudon
Campus near Paris.
Working in conjunction
with two French
development partners,
SORIF and Nexity,
Hines was selected
by Renault, the large
French automobile
manufacturer, to
purchase and develop
the site in Paris, which
is strategically located
along the banks of
the Seine River, just
southwest of the city's
center.

In Barcelona at the Diagonal Mar Centre construction site (from left): Hines senior executive Jay Wyper; Pasqual Maragall, longtime mayor of Barcelona; Gerald Hines; and Joan Clos, who was deputy mayor at the time and later became the city's mayor. The four-million-square-foot mixed-use development is located on an eighty-four-acre site in the Poble Nou seafront area.

Barcelona offered just such an ambitious challenge: Diagonal Mar Centre, a four-million-square-foot mixed-use development located on an eighty-four-acre site in the Poble Nou seafront area. Located a stone's throw from the Mediterranean, the site was purchased from another developer. Gerald Hines invested his own capital to jumpstart the project.

"We closed in September 1996, and the only key element that had value was a shopping center that had received building permissions five years earlier," says Wyper. "The permit would expire if we didn't begin construction by May 1997. But if we lost that permit we'd never get it again—they wanted to cap shopping centers in the area." Hines had several big chores: completely redesign the shopping center in a way that would not violate existing building approvals; start construction by May; and remaster the site plan with a different mix of uses, which required another phase of planning permission. If Hines didn't get the approvals and close by a specific date, they wouldn't get the funding for the project.

Meanwhile, the city and regional governments belonged to two different political parties. "One would say, 'Did the other approve it? Then we don't,'" Wyper recalls. All of the documents had to be translated into Catalan as well as Spanish. "It took eighteen months and Henry Kissinger–style diplomacy, but we got it done," Wyper says.

The construction headaches were also legion. For instance, Hines had to construct a diaphragm wall more than a half mile long and two hundred feet deep to keep the sea out of the project's first floor of retail space and five underground floors of parking—the largest garage in the country. But today, Diagonal Mar Centre is one of the largest and most prestigious developments in Europe—a three-level lifestyle center with more than 240 stores, restaurants, a multiplex theater, leisure establishments, and an Alcampo hypermarket—with a stunning view of the Mediterranean Sea.

In other countries, the issues are not structural but cultural. Hines felt the urgency to make a spectacular statement with its first major project in one of the world's most beautiful cities: Paris. Hines chose the architectural firm of Pei Cobb Freed & Partners to design the EDF Tower, a forty-story, 63,200-square-meter office building in the La Défense business district west of Paris. (Pei Cobb Freed is best known in Paris for its design of the remarkable glass pyramid addition to the Louvre.)

The building occupies a prominent site adjacent to the *dalle* of La Défense, an elevated pedestrian plaza centered on an axis that extends eastward from the nearby Grand Arche, through the Arc de Triomphe, to the courtyard of the Louvre in the heart of Paris. Hines understood the privilege of building on the site and the obligation to enhance the public space. The elegant elliptical building, clad in horizontal stripes of stainless steel and glass, features a striking conical shape carved into its northern edge. It extends from the twenty-sixth floor to the ground, where the tower's main entrance is sheltered by a wide,

circular canopy. Passersby are inspired to stand here and take in the remarkable view.

The success of the EDF Tower led Hines to another historic assignment: the purchase and redevelopment of a 110-acre site in Paris located along the banks of the River Seine, a former manufacturing facility for French automaker Renault. In conjunction with two French development partners, Hines will develop 8.75 million square feet of office, retail, residential, and public facilities over nine years. The project, named ZAC Seguin, constitutes one of the largest sites ever to be developed in Paris, particularly so close to the heart of the city.

Hines' prospects internationally are wide open. In 2006 it began exploring opportunities in India, where a burgeoning middle class is seeking quality housing and other types of real estate. If the key to Hines' international success could be summed up in a word, it would be

persistence. Says Ogilvie, "In 1990, we saw every American developer who thought he might have international instincts flying in and out of eastern European capitals. Most decided it would be too long, too hard, and too ugly to get to anything profitable, and they said, 'We're going home.' But we didn't."

Above left, Andrew Reynolds (center), a director of Hines U.K., with Hines U.K. construction director Simon Jenner (left) and architect David Warrender. The majority of Hines' international offices are managed by executives born and educated in those countries. Above, clockwise from top left, Olivier de Dampierre and Patrick Albrand, directors of Hines France; John Gomez Hall, the director of Hines Spain; and Karl Wambach, head of Hines Germany.

6

ENTREPRI

The Enterpreneurial Spirit
by William J. Poorvu

The Hines organization–fathered by Gerald Hines, and now being parented by both Gerald and his son Jeff, along with some three thousand other professionals–has reached the fifty-year mark. If a successful half-century in real estate development were a common story, the Hines organization wouldn't command our attention. But in fact, Hines is one of the few large real estate development firms to have not only survived but also prospered over five decades. So at the half-century mark, it is important to ask how Hines has achieved this singular success. ▓ The entrepreneurial spirit of one individual, Gerald Hines, helped energize an entire company–but this was more than the work of one individual. It also involved careful attention to creating a structure in which large numbers of talented people could grow. To go from being a company driven by an entrepreneur to an entrepreneurial company is not an easy step. It involves the building of trust among a myriad of external and internal players, a trust that in this case has kept its key players together for decades. ▓ Gerald Hines grew up in Depression-era Gary, Indiana, where his father was an electrical superintendent and his mother was a schoolteacher. With strong encouragement from his father, Hines studied mechanical engineering. If a Hines building is more advanced today than others in the neighborhood in terms of its engineering, this is one reason why. ▓ But after a month in an engineering lab, plotting curves and crunching numbers, Hines knew that he needed more contact with people. His personable nature was a trait that would stay with him, and help him professionally, all his life.

the side. Although insignificant in the scale of future Hines ventures, these projects introduced Hines to the fundamentals of development, including mortgage financing, design, construction, and the concepts of urban planning. He learned about the critical importance of preleasing: providing a future cash flow that could be financed. These loans—about 70 percent, on a completed-value basis—covered most of the costs. This substantially reduced the need for up-front cash, a commodity that was then in short supply in the Hines household. Hines also learned that if you made a high-quality building, you could prevail in the battle for good tenants. But this by itself, says Hines, was not enough. "I think you have to have the best interests of the tenant at heart," says Hines. "You have to provide outstanding service, and integrity, and fairness to them in the way you treat them, because many occasions come up where you have the upper hand, and you could gouge somebody. I think it's about being fair, and then having your reputation flow on from there."

Typically, tenants in those early Hines buildings didn't pay any more for these amenities; in fact, Hines took a little less. But the entrepreneur-in-the-making wasn't being altruistic. He was investing in relationships that he hoped would endure and help him in the long run.

THE HOUSTON ENTREPRENEUR
Once Hines set up his own shop in 1957, his knowledge of Houston and his prior experiences allowed him to increase the number of projects he could take on. His organization, growing slowly but surely, completed a total of eighty-five office and warehouse projects between 1957 and 1967 (out of a total portfolio of ninety-seven projects). He also expanded into other project types.

When Gerald Hines, above, was hired to sell building components out of college, he was given a choice of three different cities for his sales territory. Fortune was on his side when he chose Houston. Between 1950 and 1980, the population nearly tripled from 600,000 to 1.6 million. Opposite, One Post Oak Central in Houston, designed by Philip Johnson, was completed in 1969.

Shortly after his graduation from Purdue in 1948, Hines relocated to Houston—mainly because several of his fellow fraternity brothers were moving there. It was a stroke of luck: Houston was about to embark upon three decades of dizzying growth. Between 1950 and 1980, Houston's population nearly tripled from 600,000 to 1.6 million. In the same three decades in which Houston gained a million residents—twice as many as Dallas—New York City lost 900,000 and Chicago lost 600,000.

So Hines made a lucky choice. But he also made his own luck. He landed a partnership with Art Barnes' Texas Engineering Company, one of Houston's first mechanical engineering consulting firms. Given the hot climate of Houston and the still-novel technology of air conditioning, their business flourished.

But Hines was starting to get the real estate bug. During his five years at Texas Engineering, he built several small combined office/warehouse projects on

Over the next fifteen years, Gerald Hines learned at least four key lessons about himself, and about how his firm could do business successfully. First, Hines learned that the philosophy that had guided him in small projects could be scaled up and used for much larger projects. Building quality into a project—both in terms of mechanical sophistication and design elegance—had paid for itself on a small scale; now, the same approach was working on a much larger scale.

Second, Hines learned the value of great salesmanship. Whether by birthright or as the result of years of practice—or both—Gerald Hines turned out to be a superb salesman, especially on a one-on-one basis. He sold himself, his product, and—increasingly—his team. To cite just one example: few have taken due note of the fact that Gerald Hines himself persuaded the formidable Shell Oil Company to move its U.S. headquarters from New York to Houston. In real estate, relationships are everything. Great salespeople (with great products) tend to build great relationships—and this can lead to great results.

In putting together the Galleria, he convinced Neiman Marcus not to build a freestanding store, as was their custom at the time. Instead, they would be the sole initial retail anchor in a shopping center with an ice-skating rink—in Houston!—as the other initial anchor. It was a combination that required substantial powers of salesmanship. He also convinced several investors to put up Coca-Cola stock they did not want to sell as collateral for a bank loan that Hines could use as equity in the project. Later, as the value of the stock went up, he was able to increase the collateralized loan to meet escalating costs.

Third, Hines and his organization began rethinking their approach to project financing. Hines staked his entire net worth (about $6 million at the time) to bankroll the Galleria project (1970) and One Shell Plaza (1971), which were undertaken almost simultaneously. "If they had failed," says longtime Hines executive Louis Sklar, "we would have gone under." Hines and his colleagues decided that this bet-the-farm approach was "crazy" (Hines' term), and decided to hedge their bets on subsequent projects. Increasingly, the firm preferred to own, for example, 25 percent of a project that was well financed rather than 100 percent of a project that had 90 percent debt financing. Again, these were habits that would serve the firm well in the difficult economic times to come.

Fourth, Hines learned that real success arrived slowly. This was not a get-rich-quick business, and his success didn't arise simply because he was in the right place at the right time. In fact, it took Hines more than two decades to learn the business in Houston—a market he came to know intimately. As a direct result of this understanding, he was able to be ahead of the market and offer more to his clients and tenants. Not surprisingly, he expected his key associates to learn the business to a similar depth. Only after they did so did he feel he could trust them to make the most important decisions.

GOING NATIONAL

This was a period of explosive growth in the Hines organization as the firm grew from roughly 150 employees in the early 1970s to more than 900 in the late

1980s. Houston, at the beginning of this period, was still benefiting from the oil boom, whereas the rest of the country was suffering from high interest rates and galloping inflation.

Still, Hines realized that the range of opportunities in Houston was too limited to enable him to motivate the talented would-be entrepreneurs working for him. At the same time, he was personally excited about the prospect of taking on new and bigger challenges. For these reasons and others, he decided to see if his approach to building quality office buildings was transferable to other major cities.

He explored various ways to break into new local markets, where there were developers on the ground with more local knowledge and contacts than he had. Early on, for example, he and his associates Tom Swift and Ken Hubbard set up a banking division. By partnering with strong local financial institutions that also became lead tenants, they were able to work their way into local markets. In this way, Three First National Plaza, located in the center of Chicago's financial district, became the basis for the company's entrance into the Midwest. Hines and his colleagues played off their success in Houston to attract financial institutions that were then competing to build and occupy their own high-visibility, high-prestige signature buildings. The strategy worked.

He also went beyond the security of preleasing into more venturesome territory. The San Francisco office set up shop in 1979, and in 1980 was about to build a 1.2-million-square-foot headquarters for a California company. That client went bankrupt; Hines went ahead and completed the project in December 1982, and opened the building 95 percent leased at almost double the rents that had originally been projected.

It was a success made possible by a local economy that was thriving while Houston's was declining. As oil prices plunged, Houston developed a huge "overhang" of vacant office space. Some Hines properties were sold, and the company took on jobs for fees to keep the staff there together.

Though Gerald Hines struggled to adapt to external markets, some of his most difficult challenges were internal. Up to this point, he had implicitly embraced the "lone wolf" model of real estate entrepreneurship. "I was on every project myself," Hines later said of his Houston entrepreneurial phase. He knew everything of consequence that was going on in a project. But he realized that if he failed to expand the business beyond himself, it would never be a truly national business. The real obstacle to growth, he later observed, was not the real estate cycle, but the entrepreneur's

Gerald D. Hines has built his business methodically, thoughtfully, and by taking measured risks. Arguably his greatest risk was when he staked his entire net worth (about $6 million at the time) to bankroll the Galleria project and One Shell Plaza, which were undertaken almost simultaneously. "If they had failed," says retired Hines executive Louis Sklar, "we would have gone under."

In the 1980s, while Houston suffered under plunging oil prices, Gerald Hines turned to the thriving economy of San Francisco. After opening 101 California in 1982, he began construction on 580 California, above, which was completed in 1984. That same year, Charles Baughn, left, started with the firm. Today Baughn is executive vice president of capital markets.

chronic inability to delegate. "Oh, I think it's always people skills—and delegation," explains Hines. "And I think that's a very hard thing for an entrepreneur to do: to delegate. To learn to delegate, and trust, is a major leap that a lot of people, especially entrepreneurs, never make."

This was not something that came easily to Gerald Hines, or occurred as the result of an epiphany. He learned slowly. He learned that it was important for his partners in the field to be proud professionally of their projects and their own role in making them successful. In addition, he realized he needed to provide more of an equity incentive to his key people; otherwise, they would leave to set up their own shops. He also knew that they would perform better with a vested interest. This was both a recruitment tool—you can be an entrepreneur in the confines of a strong organization, taking on even bigger challenges and making more money than you could on your own—and a method of exercising indirect control.

Already, his key people had been with him a long time. They had learned the Hines way of doing business. For projects in which they were involved, the firm lent them the necessary capital. "They become real partners in the projects they do," Hines says. And, of course, these practices cut both ways. "And if they lose money on one, it's carried back and carried forward. So they are putting their own money on the line. I'd say that's one of the things that differentiates us: that there's substantial loss if a bad decision is made."

Hines was notably reluctant to sell buildings it constructed. The firm wanted to own for the long run. As a result of holding good buildings in key locations, the company and its associates were able to build up sizable equity stakes. Hines' example inspired new arrivals in the organization, creating a virtuous circle.

By the late 1970s, there was a clear need to impose more structure on the organization. Hines' partners found themselves bumping into one another as they tried to generate new business around the country. The banking division—with a nation-side mandate—came into conflict with the regional partners, who had been given responsibility for their areas during this period. The large size of the company (and the economic problems in Houston) also made the case for more centralized controls. In 1985, a formal executive committee was established, comprising Gerald and Jeff Hines, chief financial officer Perry Waughtal, and the regional partners. This group began meeting quarterly. Although the Hines family retained the final decision rights, the firm effectively set its strategic direction by consensus: a remarkable evolution in the life of the firm.

On the project level, the actual implementation was left to the regional managers. In those days, raising capital for a particular project was done at the local level. In some cases, the equity money came from such institutions as Deutsche Bank and the Royal Dutch Shell Pension Fund, or investors from Kuwait. They would put up the equity, and receive the bulk of the profit on a particular project. Hines would have a minor initial ownership position, with an upside based on performance. With investors such as these, many Hines projects were less leveraged and better prepared to handle the downturn that was about to come.

SURVIVING THE CYCLE

This stage in the life of the Hines organization began with a vicious national contraction in the real estate cycle: the bust of 1989. Industry-wide overspeculation and overleverage had led to a glut of supply—particularly in the Hines mainstay market of office space—and in 1989, almost overnight, the industry simply ground to a halt.

At first, the crunch mainly hurt projects that were still under development. (Because of their staggered lease expirations, existing office buildings were affected more gradually.) Here, the prior experience of having lived through Houston's economic decline served the Hines group well. They saw the crunch coming and put some projects on hold. Reluctantly, they sold a few office buildings, thereby assembling a cash reserve.

In this same time period, Hines also decided to close its industrial division. The partners had concluded that they couldn't add much value in an arena where the product was essentially a commodity, and was therefore a captive of external forces.

Despite these sometimes-painful adjustments, the Hines family and their partners were in the business for the long haul. They had seen down cycles before and wanted to position themselves to take advantage of the eventual turnaround. As they had done earlier in Houston, they undertook project management and fee development jobs for others. Much of their time was spent negotiating with existing tenants, lenders, and investors. These were not easy times, but the company fought to maintain its reputation.

In 1990, the firm made another key move in naming Jeff Hines its president. Jeff, who had joined the firm in 1981, had worked his way up through the ranks gradually and impressed his coworkers as hardworking—and not self-impressed. He

had a strong financial orientation, which his colleagues considered a good counterpoint to his visionary, project-oriented father. The fact that the two—father and son—got along well personally was a definite plus. Most important, his appointment reassured both insiders and outsiders that the firm would have the great benefit of continuity.

That same year, to reflect the new structure, the name of the company, which had been known as Gerald D. Hines Interests since its founding in 1957, was changed to Hines Interests Limited Partnership. In 1995, as the company increased its global presence, the organization began doing business simply as Hines. The firm's red logo was conceived by Houston designer Chris Hill, who wanted to create an identification that would be timeless and grow with the company. And there was another factor that facilitated the company's survival: it was privately held. As such, it could make investments with an eye toward the long term. It did not have to generate quarterly earnings for the Wall Street crowd—a circumstance that provided much-needed running room, and set the stage for future success.

ON THE GRAND SCALE

Gradually, markets absorbed the office overhang. Distressed selling on the part of financial institutions and the government wound down. Opportunities arose for those who could identify markets where rents could be raised, or where depressed prices no longer reflected a property's true economic value. But as new construction remained largely nonviable, the real value lay in acquiring existing properties at well below replacement costs.

Key executives who helped develop many of the Hines standards that are still in place today. Clockwise from top left: Perry Waughtal served as Hines' first chief financial officer. Clayton Stone was responsible for development and operations for 1100 Louisiana, the JPMorgan Chase Tower, and the Bank of America Center. Ben Franklin assisted Stone with managing a large group of young, talented project managers, among them Jeff Hines. John Harris has worked with the firm since the 1960s and pioneered its Conceptual Construction group.

For Hines, this was an entirely new ball game. In the past, the firm had been reluctant to buy other people's buildings. As Gerald Hines put it, why own properties that aren't as well constructed as our own? And on an even more fundamental level, it was more exciting to be a developer than a mere buyer and seller of properties. But the other partners understood the nature of the new game and successfully pressed the issue.

Meanwhile, the financial markets had also changed. Lenders wanted borrowers to have more of their "skin in the game"—that is, to put up 30 to 40 percent in cash. Moreover, they only wanted to do business with companies that had come through the downturn with their reputations intact. Hines met that test easily, but like most real estate firms, much of its equity was illiquid.

And the lenders had changed. Commercial banks and insurance companies had pulled back. But on the positive side, many pension and endowment funds—such as the General Motors Pension Fund and CalPERS, which had experienced some losses in the stock market—were anxious to allocate more funds to real estate. The downside for Hines was that the company now had investment partners who might demand a bigger role in decision-making—which was uncomfortable for a decentralized entrepreneurial culture in which the partners were accustomed to making most decisions on their own. They could still make hiring decisions in their area and allocate their regions' ownership interests to members of their team. They still ran the operating side of their projects and took pride in the fact that neither Gerald nor Jeff called into question their real estate judgment.

Now, though, they had to adapt their focus to a new business, acquiring and adding value to existing properties, and finding new ways to raise capital. Given the company's strong reputation, Hines was soon able to establish its own funds by amalgamating investments from a number of institutions. This gave them more investment flexibility—but at the same time, a greater fiduciary responsibility. The company had to manage the inherent conflict of being the promoter—the recipient of fees for services or performance-based fees—with its obligation to maximize returns to its investors. This conflict also further changed the relationship between the Houston headquarters and the regional offices. Regional partners were now more dependent upon Central to find funds and allocate them to their projects. In the decade prior, relationships had been key in dealing with investment partners. Now processes—prescribed interactions with institutions—became more of an issue.

The company took these added fiduciary responsibilities seriously. Each fund had its own manager in Houston who negotiated with the regional partners on individual projects. These negotiations, according to some who participated in them, were not always easy, in part because regional partners' profits were based on projects in which they were involved. As the company grew, headquarters' role in monitoring design, construction, and operating standards also became more important.

For all that, Hines realized the importance of maintaining the entrepreneurial spirit of its partners and regions. Too often, the combination of size, bureaucracy, and change of direction can destroy the heart of a company. The bigger the company and the faster it grows, the more likely that it will have trouble finding the proper organizational structure, devising a fair compensation system, and defining an appropriate degree of delegation.

So the Houston headquarters, now headed by Jeff Hines and chief financial officer Hasty Johnson, had to assume a greater role, which meant it had to attract great people at the core. As a result, a portion of the profit sharing on each fund was apportioned to Houston. To make all of this work, the Hines family, spearheaded by Jeff, reduced the family's percentage of ownership and simultaneously encouraged regional partners to expand the number of people who were eligible to share from their pot.

Louis Sklar (second from right) with Hines employees Bob Clark (right) and Becky Dossey. Hines has retained much of the spirit and mission of the firm founded by Gerald Hines in 1957. It remains committed to constructing buildings of superior quality, providing high levels of tenant service at a reasonable cost, and treating the people inside and outside the firm with respect and integrity.

The entrepreneurial spirit is evident in the Hines employees who blazed new trails into international markets. Above, Gonzalo Cortabarria (left), Steve Dolman (middle), and Doug Munro comprised Hines' first team in South America. Left, Lee Timmins, who relocated to Moscow in 1993 and was responsible for Hines' first joint venture in eastern Europe that same year.

During this period, the company took another major step forward: it decided to go international in a big way. Gerald Hines had always been eager to go that route, and he had been testing the waters for years with more or less ambitious projects in places such as Canada and Mexico. But now, with a decline in development opportunities in the U.S., the shortage of first-class space in Europe, and the emergence of many developing countries, the time appeared right to make a major push. The company could bring its technical and development experience, plus its access to Western capital, to these areas.

How Hines went about this is a fascinating story. Rather than set up a new independent international division, the company assigned each U.S. regional partner an area of the world to investigate. This made international expansion central to the company's future and reinvigorated the excitement level of the regional partners. These partners had to figure out which markets were most appropriate, define which products would best fit local needs, set up and staff local offices, and actually make deals. Since partners looked at these offices as their creations and stood to gain financially from what happened in their international areas, they encouraged members of their own teams to spend time abroad working toward these objectives.

The push to go international was enthusiastically encouraged by the Hines family in a number of ways. First, Gerald himself was excited at the prospect of new frontiers, and—in the mid-1990s—he moved to Europe to help development efforts there. Michael Topham moved to Europe from Chicago to set up the offices. Again, being a private company worked in Hines'

favor. The Hines family was willing to open—and staff at a high level—offices that would take years to become profitable, in the interest of making sure that what those offices offered and produced was at a Hines-level quality.

This was easier said than done. Finding the right local managers and training them to "think like a Hines person" could take years. The product had to be adapted to local conditions. "The point is to build what the market wants," as Topham puts it, "and to build a sustainable business." The results were impressive: more than one hundred offices in fourteen countries, and growth from about one thousand employees in the 1980s and early 1990s to about three thousand in 2006. The Hines organization became a full-fledged, border-crossing operation.

Moreover, this occurred at about the same time Hines was becoming a multi-generational family business. Against long odds, it got the benefits of both without incurring the evils of either. Consider Gerald Hines' response when he is asked what "family business" means to him: "We're very responsive to the individuals who have pledged their loyalty to our firm. And we go out of our way to make sure that if bad things happen to them in any way, we're there. And I think that we can do things that others can't—as we did in the early 1990s, when the downturn came. Other firms laid off 25 to 50 percent of their people; we didn't lay off anyone. We kept them by getting development management and property management work, and by digging deep into our own pockets. And when the turnaround came, we were there with an outstanding organization."

But it wasn't just a case of taking the long view. By relocating to Europe, for example, Gerald not only refocused his own still-prodigious energies on entrepreneurial

pursuits, but also gave Jeff more visibility, authority, and critical running room within the U.S.-based organization.

MATTERS OF TRUST

The Hines organization has survived, grown, and prospered over the past fifty years. It is one of the few real estate development organizations to have done so. Its entrepreneurial spirit has fostered a culture that has led the company to take advantage of new opportunities without overextending itself and thereby becoming swamped by the periodic downturns of a cyclical industry.

In some fundamental ways, the firm today is similar to the one that was born in 1957 when Gerald Hines opened his main office in Houston. The firm's mission has remained constant: to build better buildings, to provide a high level of service at a reasonable cost to its tenants, to treat those with whom it does business with respect and integrity, and to make a fair profit for itself and its investors. So there is a consistency of vision, which trumps what would otherwise appear to be a morphing into a totally different animal.

It's tempting to ascribe that consistency of vision to the most visible constant factor: Gerald Hines himself. But instilling an entrepreneurial spirit is not just an issue of individual leadership. It involves getting the controls, organization, delegation of responsibilities, and compensation system right. Effective entrepreneurship involves hard work.

Entrepreneurs too often fall victim to thinking that they personally will be able to convince others to see the light, and come

Franck Laget (left)
and Aurore Mensch
in Hines' Paris office.
Founded in 1995,
the office has since
completed the Havas
Headquarters in
Suresnes, France,
and the 103-room
Hôtel Villiers-Ampère,
the EDF Tower, the
M6 Headquarters
renovation, and the
CB16 Tower renovation
in Paris. By 2006,
Hines France had
completed over
193,300 square meters
of commercial property.

Gerald Hines, shown above, skiing, is still actively involved in the company he founded. At right, Hines is pictured with executive Hasty Johnson (right), who each year organizes a ski trip that gives selected young associates the privilege of spending time with their firm's founder.

around to their point of view. As a rule, it's not true, and it's not possible. Setting ground rules and building an organization are crucial to sustained growth, and few firms have responded adequately to those challenges. Changing supply and demand forces, regulatory pressures, and financial markets require a company to be flexible and adaptable. This is a cyclical industry with new configurations of players. The importance of the fact that much of the senior Hines team has worked together for decades cannot be overstated.

The Hines organization has adapted, in part, by developing and maintaining auxiliary businesses that complement the company's property management activities. Over the years, Hines has operated construction, cleaning, elevator, locksmith, parking, and security businesses "because we could not find third-party vendors in those categories that could deliver the quality we were accustomed to providing to our customers," explains Hines vice president of operations Cliff Gann.

Although the companies are profitable, profit was not Hines' primary motivation in entering these fields, explains Gann. "We were just fed up with the service we were getting and thought, We can do it better ourselves." Gerald Hines has encouraged his organization to act on instincts like those.

Not that the Hines organization hasn't made mistakes over the years. In fact, it has—in part because many decisions have been made not as part of a grand strategy but in response to some unexpected opportunity or crisis. But many of these decisions ultimately turned out right for the wrong reasons. And as noted, there was always the factor of luck: being in the right place at the right time. (In 1952, Houston was poised for explosive growth; in later decades it was not.) But when a company somehow has guessed right more often than not, over this long a period, we should assume that there's something more than "luck" at work, and that there's much we can learn about how the Hines organization has gone about its business.

Real estate entrepreneurship at any level requires creating the right product/market mix; gaining the necessary approvals; assembling, motivating, and rewarding the right team to carry out a project; and providing adequate debt and equity capital with the proper time frame. This is essentially a project business, and that is where most entrepreneurs get their kicks. At the same time, in order to grow as Hines has, the challenge has been to balance this enthusiasm with the central controls that keep the enterprise as a whole from overextending.

What of Gerald Hines himself? As of this writing, he continues to practice his true passion: pursuing deals and making them happen. He still serves as an inspirational figure and sage counselor to the larger organization. For example, he takes part in trips organized by Hasty Johnson—the most recent being a ski trip off the coast of Norway in the spring of 2006—that give selected young associates the privilege of spending time with their firm's founder, and seeing firsthand how much an octogenarian blessed with good health and a still-fascinating career can enjoy life. It also points to one of the key challenges the company faces for its future: transmitting to the next generation its entrepreneurial spirit, thereby instilling in future associates the confidence that Hines is a firm where they should commit their careers.

The key has been establishing a culture of trust—not only among the people with whom Hines does business, but also among the people within the organization. Real estate is an enormously fragmented business in which it is relatively easy to switch firms or go out on one's own. So it's critical to build trust—trust that the leadership will find opportunities, put together the resources to carry them out, attract and manage great people, and treat the people within the organization fairly.

This trust must be earned continuously. Hines has done so, and that goes a long way toward explaining why the organization is still celebrating its success after fifty years.

7

ARCHIT

PAR

SHOP

I N G

PLAZA / SKATING

LIFT

1" = 20'-0"

ASPEN HIGHLANDS
RAMSA — SECTION/ELEV.
8/6/92   1"=20'

TECT

The Architect Relationship
by David Childs

As extraordinary as were the Medici's contributions to Renaissance art and architecture, so too is Gerald Hines' statement–implicit in every building he commissions–that architecture is important, not only practically, but artistically. While the construction of speculative buildings later became the typical developer's bread and butter, Hines was developing buildings solely on spec at a time when this was relatively rare. Those actions speak to his profound belief in and affinity for the power of architecture to change the way cities and their inhabitants grow. ▦ Hines' attention to architecture has been good not only for the profession, but also for urbanism, as has been his unwavering concern for the quality his buildings extend–beyond the plot of land and the frame of the site–to the community. Unlike so many developers who come in and build with minimal nods to their unique urban context, Hines went so far as to open regional offices in cities such as Atlanta, Chicago, New York, and San Francisco. Many of the offices were initially tied to specific projects, and it was this focus on developing an actual relationship with the community–as well as a building–that proved so crucial. What was important to the locals, then, became important to the company. ▦ Hines not only understands the importance of context, but he also remains truly committed to the creation of contextual architecture. And it is this focus, this attention to detail, and this unerring commitment to developing buildings that are good from the inside out and the landscape in, that sets Gerald Hines–and his company–apart.

A MODERN-DAY MEDICI

In an era of big booms and big buildings, Hines is one of the rare developers who takes the time to derive personal pleasure from the art of architecture. For him, buildings aren't simply rentable spaces, empty shells, structures comprehensible only in terms of the number of square feet to be sold, the caliber of tenants to be acquired, the amount of profit to be gleaned. For Hines, as for all developers, these are considerations, but they are by no means tantamount. Architecture is equally important. And as business-savvy and economically successful as this elevation of design later proved to be, Hines' early focus on working with architects to create architecture that stands alone and says something beyond "Buy me!" or "Rent me!" is as close to pure as possible. Ada Louise Huxtable, writing years ago but already the last-word critic she is today, once called Hines a "modern-day Medici," a compelling comparison to that most ancient and artistically aware family who focused not only their money but their energies on supporting the creation of excellence in art and architecture.

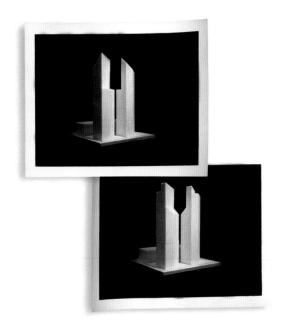

Pennzoil Place, above, marked a turning point in the notable career of Philip Johnson, who before Hines' invitation to design the building had done almost no work for commercial developers. With its dual towers separated by glass-covered lobbies, it also represented a turning point in post-war public architecture. Left, models show Johnson's alternate ideas for topping off Pennzoil Place.

HINES AS CLIENT

The relationship between an architect and his client is often friendly, sometimes tense, but always complex. In a world that thrives equally on the creative spark, the myth of the genius architect, and the logistical details of constructing a building—one of the most complicated, difficult, and time-consuming creative undertakings—a good relationship with a client is hard to come by, and of immeasurable value. Just as there is nothing worse than a bad client, there's nothing better than a good one—one who is there not only to sign the checks and sign off on the drawings, but who collaborates, who understands, who can read the blueprints and imagine the building, who challenges the architect to do his best work, and then, when all is said and done, ensures that the building that exists in the architect's mind can become a reality. In popular architectural culture, the myth (and sadly, often reality) of the client as antagonistic patron continues to exist, expand, and devour the few clients who have risen to the top of their game not through cutthroat mechanics and Machiavellian operations, but because

they alone understand that while capital-A Architecture can stand on its own in conception, it needs help with the translation into reality. Gerald Hines is one of these rare clients.

Hines swept into Washington, D.C., in the 1970s, an era when Nat Owings, Senator Pat Moynihan, and I were working on the plan for the Washington Mall and development was rampant, almost to the point of running wild. The commercial market there was not yet so saturated that

buildings needed to somehow qualify as "architectural" just to be noticed; rather, D.C. at that time was so open that anything could go up and the developer could lease it. That was where I met Hines. I was struck by his interest in architecture, but more so by his willingness to follow through and put his money, quite literally, where his buildings were. In Washington, Hines began to make his mark as a novel sort of developer—one who cared as much about creating quality architecture as the architect did. That was something that had rarely—if ever—been seen before in modern American commercial construction. And in caring so much for his buildings, and showing so much interest in the art of architecture, he hit upon what would become his secret weapon and, indeed, his legacy: he began to build better buildings than the competition.

Even in that strong Washington, Hines' developments—the Robert A. M. Stern–designed 600 Thirteenth Street, Pei Cobb Freed's Columbia Square, and the Philip Johnson/John Burgee creation Franklin Square—began to stand out. Slowly but surely, the people who were in charge

Philip Johnson and John Burgee

Philip Johnson and John Burgee were among the earliest and most frequent collaborators with Gerald Hines, who turned to their firm for its iconic postmodern style. Johnson—who won the prestigious Pritzker Architecture Prize in 1979—studied architectural history at Harvard and founded the Department of Architecture and Design at the Museum of Modern Art in New York before returning to Harvard for his master's degree in architecture. In 1967, Johnson joined forces with Burgee, an architect with extensive experience managing large projects, and began a twenty-year partnership that catapulted their status in the world of commercial architecture. Johnson and Burgee's projects for Hines include Post Oak Central (now 5051 Westheimer), Pennzoil Place, Williams Tower, and Bank of America Center in Houston; Wells Fargo Center in Denver; Five Hundred Boylston in Boston; 101 California and 580 California in San Francisco; 53rd At Third in New York City; 1180 Peachtree in Atlanta; Franklin Square in Washington, D.C.; and Comerica Tower at Detroit Center.

of leasing buildings, the people who in the boardrooms and behind the scenes had power over the way the city developed, began catching on. It might not have been Hines' intention to create an entirely new developer environment that prized good architecture and ignored the bad, but it was certainly the result.

THE COLLABORATIVE SPIRIT

Over the years, Skidmore, Owings & Merrill (SOM) has worked with Hines in cities from Miami to Houston to New York to Norwalk, Connecticut. Our first big project together dates back to 1971 with the completion of Houston's One Shell Plaza, at the time the tallest reinforced concrete structure in the world. The "tube within a tube" engineering of One Shell Plaza pushed the limits of construction technologies and created a new benchmark in its bold use of that ubiquitous material—an ambitious move that was made possible through what can only be called Hines' visionary stance: his willingness to trust SOM's experimental and forward-thinking approach, coupled with SOM's willingness to trust Hines to see this challenging project through to successful completion. One Shell Plaza was a perfect symbiosis of an architect's daring and a developer's support. It set the stage for later shared efforts, from Two Shell Plaza, also in Houston, to the 1984 construction of the Southeast (now Wachovia) Financial Center in Miami; 225 High Ridge Road in Stamford, Connecticut; Chemed Center at 255 Fifth in Cincinnati; and 450 Lexington and 383 Madison Avenue in New York City.

Skidmore, Owings & Merrill

Founded in 1936, Skidmore, Owings & Merrill LLP (SOM) is one of the world's leading architecture firms. SOM has completed projects in forty countries, and is perhaps best known for the design and construction of the Sears Tower in Chicago. The firm has a lengthy history with Hines, beginning with One Shell Plaza in Houston in 1971, the tallest reinforced concrete structure in the world at the time. Other collaborations include Two Shell Plaza and 1100 Louisiana in Houston; One Shell Square in New Orleans; 450 Lexington and 383 Madison Avenue in New York City; the Wachovia Financial Center in Miami; PNC Center and Chemed Center at 255 Fifth in Cincinnati; 225 High Ridge Road in Stamford, Connecticut; and Three First National Plaza in Chicago.

Bear Stearns world headquarters at 383 Madison Avenue, at Madison and 47th Street in New York City. Designed by Skidmore, Owings & Merrill, the 757-foot-tall structure is clad in light-colored Deer Isle granite, lightly tinted glass and silver-painted metal trim. An architectural glass crown, designed by artist Jamie Carpenter, is illuminated from within.

Richard Tomlinson, one of SOM's managing partners, began working on speculative projects with Gerald Hines in the 1970s, and served as the lead architect in Hines' wholesale renovation of the John Portman–designed GM Renaissance Center in Detroit, which was completed in 2006. "He was really one of the first developers who, from a commercial development standpoint, made good architecture a marketing advantage," Tomlinson says from his Chicago office. "He did stone buildings when no one was doing stone buildings. He was doing high-quality restroom facilities, superior hardware, plazas, and parks. He had a

commitment to art, and he commissioned it. This was his difference." Tomlinson is quick to point out that Hines' commitment wasn't solely commercial but altruistic as well. "It was both," he says. "I think he was trying to make a difference, and he had a genuine interest. He believed in it."

Hines' strength is in collaborating with the design team on all levels, down to the nuts and bolts. "A lot of the focus was on doing structural systems much more economically, so that we could save time and construction money, all of which accrued to the benefit of the projects," Tomlinson explains. "They got tenants in faster, and then they'd take those savings and turn them into architectural differentiation."

Adrian Smith, who also works in SOM's Chicago office, states that Hines is "simply and indisputably the greatest developer of the twentieth century." When asked what is so special about Hines, Smith remembers, "In the 1960s and '70s, Gerry was a real pioneer in the development of commercial buildings that had architectural integrity, which was unique among developers of that time." More than that, Hines was "very personally involved with every detail in his early work." Rather than signing a contract

Norman Foster

Known for his sleek minimalism and attention to detail, Englishman Norman Foster received his master's degree from the Yale School of Architecture in 1962. Two years later, he caused a sensation with his Cornwall building, the "Cockpit"–a glass bubble partially dug into the ground. It was followed by countless sophisticated designs, including the Swiss Re tower in London in 2004, which the *Wall Street Journal* called "the most ingenious and elegant new skyscraper built anywhere in the world for at least thirty years." Foster collaborated with Hines to design the Metropolitan, an award-winning multiuse office building in Warsaw, Poland, facing historic Pilsudski Square and adjacent to the National Opera House. Foster was knighted in 1990 and made Lord Foster of Thames Bank in 1999–the same year he won the Pritzker Architecture Prize.

Hines and architect Norman Foster brought a new standard of building systems and finishes to Warsaw with Metropolitan, a multiuse office building on historic Pilsudski Square. It includes nearly 400,000 square feet of office, and 37,000 square feet of retail and services. Hines completed the building in 2003 and sold it in 2006.

In 1998, Hines purchased a twenty-one-story office building located in Mexico City's plaza of the Angel of Independence, Mexico's best known monument. The building was in need of extensive renovation, and Hines selected Robert A. M. Stern as the renovation architect for the project. The renewed Class A office tower is now known as Torre del Angel.

and disappearing, Hines "spent a lot of time with his architects and contributed his knowledge about what would and would not rent," points out Smith. Smith worked with Hines on a 1.4-million-square-foot project, the Three First National Plaza building in Chicago. "By this time, Gerry had become emancipated from the building as a box," he says, "and could see the marketability of special shapes in architecture."

Robert A. M. Stern owes much of his early success to Hines' collaborative spirit. "The thing about Gerry is that he really likes architecture," Stern says from his New York City office. Stern first worked with Hines in the early 1980s when he still hadn't

designed anything bigger than a house. Gerry offered him an office building. As Stern tells the story, the others who were working on the project were a bit more skeptical than Hines. "They said to Gerry, 'How can you ask Stern to do an office when he's never done one before?'" he remembers. "Gerry responded, 'Stern can design, and you guys know how to put an office building together.'"

TAKING RISKS

Stern calls Hines' style a "basic risk-taking approach."

"He doesn't see architects, or anyone, in narrow boxes. And he doesn't want the same building twice from the same architect either." Rather, "he wants each problem solved on its own terms, which makes him very special."

The two collaborated on a ski resort in Aspen, Colorado. In the early design stages, rather than poring over plans and sketches, Hines took Stern on a week-long trip through Switzerland and France. "When you travel for seven days together—including the Alps, where we got caught in an avalanche—you get to know people pretty well," Stern points out. "That's how Gerry likes to work." Hines, Stern says, "wants to look, he wants to see, but he doesn't just want to do it himself and come back with a bunch of pictures." To truly collaborate on a resort project, it was essential to Hines that architect and

Robert A. M. Stern

From Boston to Barcelona, Robert A. M. Stern has created architecture that resonates with the historic and natural environment. Stern, principal of the New York firm that bears his name and dean of the Yale School of Architecture, has been involved in vast urban planning projects including Hines' Diagonal Mar in Barcelona, an eighty-four-acre development including office, residential, hotel, and retail space, and a public park. Other projects with Hines include 600 Thirteenth Street in Washington, D.C.; Torre Almirante in Brazil; Two Twenty Two Berkeley in Boston; Torre del Angel in Mexico City; and the planned communities of Aspen Highlands and River Valley Ranch in Colorado.

developer see inspiration together. "We went to examine and exchange ideas, and to try and figure out what made certain resorts work."

The architect Cesar Pelli has also worked on a number of projects with Hines. "It's a pleasure to work with Gerry because he's so intelligent," Pelli says. "The discussions I have with him, the dialogue, the searching for appropriate strategies to achieve our common goals, always take place on a very high plane." For Pelli, collaborating with Hines on buildings like the Wells Fargo Center in Minneapolis,

the Porta Nuova project in Milan, or an office building for Boston's South Station, has always proved to be a highly creative process. More typically minded developers, Pelli points out, are often less interested in design and tend to see it as "something extra that is frivolous." Not so with Hines.

"They are so knowledgeable and clear-headed," Pelli says of the people who make up Hines' firm. Through the efforts of Hines' employees, the company continues to carry on the architecturally inclined traditions honed by its founder. "He was the first one

to realize that good design has value; it's not treated like that by everybody, " he says. "With Hines, the design will be protected, even through the value engineering," said Pelli. It's a protection, Pelli points out, that can't be taken for granted. Pelli worked with Hines on the Owens Corning company's world headquarters in Toledo, Ohio, and once again was grateful for the developer's deeper understanding of the real value of architecture. "We had a restricted budget," he remembers. "It would have been extremely difficult to achieve without Hines—they were able to help us use every dollar very intelligently." And while the architect acknowledges that the project "would have been difficult—or impossible!—without Gerry," Pelli's close collaboration with Hines' son Jeffrey confirmed his beliefs that Gerald Hines has cemented his values in the corporation that carries his name.

Cesar Pelli

Born and raised in Argentina, architect Cesar Pelli is best known for his striking Petronas Twin Towers in Malaysia, which were the world's tallest buildings until 2004. Pelli began his career in the office of renowned modernist architect Eero Saarinen and has also served as dean of Yale's School of Architecture. In 1991, the American Institute of Architects listed him as one of the ten most influential living American architects. Pelli's work for Hines includes Edificio Coca-Cola and Del Bosque in Mexico City; the JPMorgan Chase Building in San Francisco; the Wells Fargo Center in Minneapolis; 1100 Louisiana in Houston; 30 Hudson in Jersey City, New Jersey; the Owens Corning World Headquarters in Toledo, Ohio; and Porta Nuova, a massive urban planning project in Milan.

A Cesar Pelli project takes shape: the Owens Corning World Headquarters in Toledo, Ohio, from architectural sketches, right, to computer-modeled site plan, below, to reality, above.

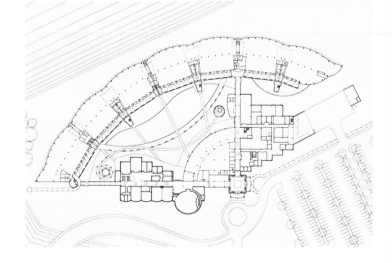

Architect Frank Gehry and the evolution of his ideas. Numerous sketches and models evolve to computer-generated plans as Gehry develops whimsical structures like the conference hall inside DZ Bank in Berlin, Germany, left.

It is clear that Pelli is most inspired by the way that Hines embraces collaborative relationships, especially when working on projects for third-party clients. With those projects, he points out, "you don't have to please only Hines, but we work together with Hines to please the occupier of the building." In those cases, the relationship is far more complex. "They are our clients, but at the same time we are collaborators," Pelli says.

On another side of architectural style is Frank Gehry, who worked with Hines on DZ Bank in Berlin, Germany. A stunning centerpiece of the building is a conference room often called the "Horse's Head," a signature Gehry swooping shape that takes up the center atrium and always makes one wonder how Gehry managed to build it. The answer is, with Hines. Hines' role in the project also explains why the bank, which was a partner with Hines, was willing to hire an architect who, though tested, was still working on a construction level above and beyond much of what was going on around him. "The Hines people were on the selection committee, and probably realized that we had some talent, that we knew what we were doing. They probably pointed it out," Gehry says from his LA office,

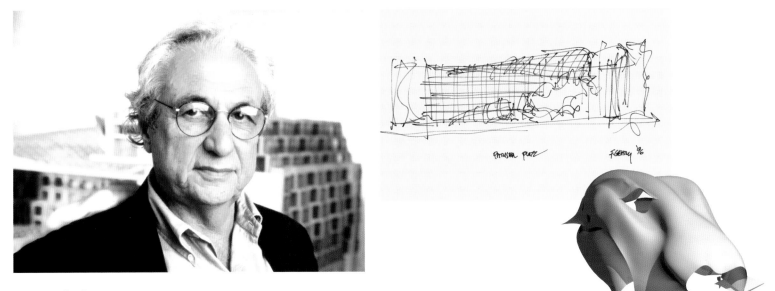

Frank Gehry

Frank Gehry is admired for his modern sculptural designs, primal geometric surfaces, and use of nontraditional building materials. The 1989 winner of the Pritzker Architecture Prize, Gehry has been designing from Los Angeles under his own name since the 1960s. He is best known for the Guggenheim Museum in Bilboa, a complex of interconnecting organic shapes in titanium and glass. Gehry partnered with Hines to produce the DZ Bank building at Pariser Platz 3 in Berlin, an office and residential complex across from the Brandenburg Gate. The building features a classical façade of glass and Italian limestone, but inside it gives way to an audacious glass-covered interior courtyard and free-form conference area shaped like the skull of a prehistoric horse. The project was featured in the Sydney Pollack documentary *Sketches of Frank Gehry*. Hines managed the construction economics of bringing Gehry's vision for the Walt Disney Concert Hall in Los Angeles to fruition. Hines and Gehry partnered again to develop a concert hall for the New World Symphony in Miami, scheduled to open in 2010.

Kevin Roche designed Ravinia, an eco-friendly office/hotel complex, left, in 1985. It was Hines' first foray into the Atlanta real estate market. Roche designed a master plan, opposite top, to encompass the natural topography of the site, including gardens, walking trails, streams, waterfalls, and a lake. Opposite bottom, a rendering for another Hines-Roche collaboration, 31 West 52nd Street in New York City.

where he is designing a Miami concert hall that is being project-managed by Hines. "It was clear from our model that we knew what we were doing," he says, "but it took somebody like them to recognize it." In fact, the Hines-Gehry collaboration in Berlin is so emblematic of the architect's singular style that the building was featured in the climactic final scene of Sydney Pollack's 2006 documentary on Gehry.

"STARCHITECTURE"
Hines' unique method of working with architects goes back a long time and a long way into architectural history. "When he did that early work in Houston with

Philip Johnson, it was mind-boggling that a developer understood architects," Gehry says. "It's an old story that architects create value, but it got forgotten for a few years." Gehry pins the midcentury blankness of architecture on a post-war mentality. "People's minds were on survival, so buildings were built with the idea of efficiency and saving money. They were very spare and sparse, and were just about getting it done." Finally, he says, things changed, but not without a little help. "Then came a period of thinking that there had to be something more to this game.' And then along came Hines with Philip, and they developed a model in Houston of a building that's capital-A Architecture."

That moment, Gehry argues, "hit on all cylinders." More importantly, he says, "it was the Hines vision that brought it to reality." Pennzoil Place in Houston "was

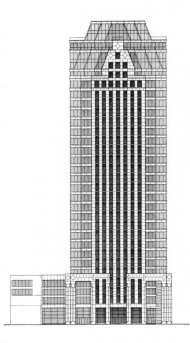

Kevin Roche

In the spring of 1950, Irish-born architect Kevin Roche joined Eero Saarinen and Associates, becoming Saarinen's principal design associate. When Saarinen died in 1961, Roche took over the practice with John Dinkeloo, who had been in charge of production documents. Together, they completed a dozen major projects for the firm before launching their own Connecticut-based company, Kevin Roche John Dinkeloo and Associates. In 1982, Roche won the Pritzker Architecture Prize. Roche's landmark work includes the Ford Foundation Headquarters and an expansion of the Metropolitan Museum of Art in New York City and the Oakland Museum of California. For Hines, Roche designed the E. F. Hutton Building (now occupied by Deutsche Bank) at 31 West 52nd Street, a granite and glass skyscraper with a unique, Byzantine lobby.

the first model, and when those of us in architecture looked at it, we thought, 'There's a guy that really gets it—and is ready to do something about it.'" That, Gehry says, was a turning point for the profession. "That opened the door, and I think a lot of people followed through after that. But certainly Gerry was the first to do that stuff. And we all noticed it, and all appreciated it."

Stern agrees that without Hines, the architect-client landscape would be a very different one indeed. "He has set the standard and raised the bar," Stern says. "So many other developers now are quite committed and realize the value of having an architect whose name is on the project, but even more than that, produces something that can be described as a high-profile product." That said, Hines was not only a marketing whiz—he was a true fan of architecture. "I don't think Gerry ever sold the architect's name so much as the actual building," Stern says. With his collaborative approach and architectural knowledge, it's clear that Hines never had to.

In the past decade, there has been a marked shift in the dynamics of the architect-client relationship within the residential real estate community. Where once typically big-name developers overshadowed their smaller-name architects on well-marketed but sometimes hastily designed condominium buildings, now it is de rigueur for smaller developers to hire "star" architects for their high-profile (and far better-designed) projects. Office towers have always and will always be able to garner attention simply by virtue of their massive scale and economic necessity, but the quality of the current crop of residential towers can be attributed to a new culture-wide attention to architecture that echoes what Hines helped to foster on the commercial front.

Big-name architects now help to sell a building in a way unheard of before Hines ushered in this new era of iconic starchitecture. For example, when the Hearst Corporation decided to build a

Pei Cobb Freed & Partners

Since its formation in 1955, Pei Cobb Freed & Partners (formerly I. M. Pei & Partners) has become a master of modernist architecture, completing more than two hundred projects in over one hundred cities worldwide. The firm's clients have included major corporations, private developers, and public authorities, and its projects have comprised the expansion of the Louvre Museum in Paris, New York City's Four Seasons Hotel, and the Rock and Roll Hall of Fame in Cleveland, Ohio. Projects for Hines include the JPMorgan Chase Tower in Houston; the EDF Tower, a forty-story office building in Paris; and Columbia Square in Washington, D.C., an early leader in environmentally sustainable architecture designed by cofounder Henry Cobb. Cofounder I. M. Pei won the Pritzker Architecture Prize in 1983.

The EDF Tower in Paris, designed by Pei Cobb Freed & Partners and completed in May 2001, is a narrow structure of glass and stainless steel. The site is adjacent to the *dalle* of La Défense, an elevated pedestrian plaza centered on the axis that extends eastward from the nearby Grande Arche, through the Arc de Triomphe, to the courtyard of the Louvre in the heart of Paris. Passersby marvel at the building's wide, circular canopy. Left: Sketches of EDF's circular canopy.

Tour EDF · Paris · La Défense · 2001

Hines

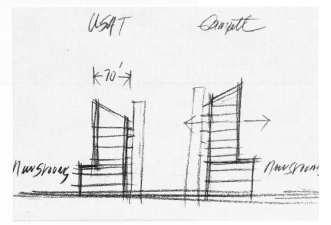

Kohn Pedersen
Fox designed the
Gannett/USA TODAY
Headquarters on a
twenty-five-acre site
near Washington,
D.C.'s Beltway. Instead
of building a single
high-rise to house the
newspaper and its
parent company, the
firm split the complex
into two angled glass
units that flow together,
both inside and out.

new headquarters in midtown Manhattan, they hired Lord Norman Foster. A British architect respected for his super-high-tech work, Foster had collaborated with Hines on the Metropolitan building in Warsaw. The newly constructed *New York Times* building, similarly high-profile, is currently under construction and was designed by Renzo Piano, another internationally acclaimed architect. Foster and Piano have become household names, recognized by people who, without the architectural climate nurtured by Hines, might never have stopped to notice.

In New York City particularly, the residential landscape—once only sparsely

supplied with notable buildings—has become virtually swamped by a seemingly continuous construction of heretofore unprecedented quality and scope. Consider the scene downtown: a new Gwathmey Siegel condo development in the East Village is a twenty-minute walk from a series of Richard Meier towers that overlook the Hudson River, as does Philip Johnson's Urban Glass House, a (posthumous) collaboration with Annabelle Selldorf. To their north is the new office building that Frank Gehry has designed for Barry Diller's IAC/InterActiveCorp. Hines has also contributed to the trend with 40 Mercer, a Jean Nouvel–designed condo in SoHo. It can be easy to take for granted that a city like New York has so much great architecture in one place, but we must remember that it was not so long ago that developers would have resisted hiring someone as forward-thinking and creative as any of those architects.

The spirit that Hines put in motion with his early and ambitious buildings lives on in these projects today; it is, in a sense, his

legacy. By celebrating architecture, and by fostering its continued growth as an art form, Hines has helped to popularize the high-designed commercial building without losing any of its essential qualities to the rigors of the mass market. Those enlightened developers—willing, for instance, to stand behind Meier's minimalist glass boxes or Gwathmey's undulating icon—might not have been so amenable to such experiments had Hines' success not paved the way. The willingness to spend an extra dollar, or a million, to ensure that the cityscape is one that speaks to its citizens and its visitors, is a remarkable quality in a developer.

Kohn Pedersen Fox Associates

Kohn Pedersen Fox Associates was founded in 1976 by A. Eugene Kohn, William Pedersen, and Sheldon Fox. Their award-winning work, primarily focused in urban settings, covers a wide spectrum of design, from the building of a jewel-like glass pavilion for Rodin sculptures to the creation of an entire city in Incheon, Korea. The firm is known for its collaborative approach and for designs that respond to their environment in terms of context and sustainability. Hines has worked with the firm's London-based president, Lee Polisano, on several global projects. With Hines, Kohn Pedersen Fox Associates has designed structures including the office tower 191 North Wacker in Chicago; the Mitretek Systems headquarters in Falls Church, Virginia; Benrather Karree, a mixed-used development in Düsseldorf, Germany; and CB16 Tower in Paris.

8 INNOVATION

INNOVATION

Construction on the Texas Commerce Tower in Houston in 1981, now known as the JPMorgan Chase Tower. Designed by I. M. Pei, the seventy-five-story structure remains Houston's tallest building. It is also the tallest granite-clad building in the world, and the world's tallest composite concrete and steel building.

Equipment in Hines buildings usually outlasts normal life cycles. At One Shell Plaza, the centrifugal chillers for the air conditioning system are still in place, due to the quality and frequency of maintenance. The equipment operates at the same level of efficiency as it did when it was brand new.

Innovation
by Ron Nyren

The world's tallest light concrete structure. Full-height doors. Groundbreaking marketing centers. Bringing iconic architects to the commercial arena. No other commercial real estate developer has given the industry as many innovations as the company founded by Gerald Hines. And that legacy of inventiveness is firmly rooted. ▣ "It has just become the firm culture, to be creative," says Jeffrey Hines, president of Hines and son of Gerald. "And now all these innovations that we are doing, in terms of incorporating sustainable design and sharing best practices—they're all a legacy of what Dad and a few others put in place many years ago." ▣ How can one of the world's largest real estate development companies also remain one of the most innovative for so long? The first and most important reason is the character of its founder, Gerald Hines. What has compelled him to be so inventive? John Harris, executive vice president of Conceptual Construction at Hines, who has worked with Gerald since the 1960s, says, "It's in Gerry's nature, his personality. I think from the first small warehouse building he developed, he always wanted to be the best." Unlike many developers, whose backgrounds are in finance, Gerald Hines is a degreed mechanical engineer. His training gave him a penchant for paying close attention to the details, right down to the design of a canopy or the details of a cornice. "I think Gerry was always an architect at heart," Harris says. "The pleasure of making a great building—something that endures, something that you can point out to your children many years later—is central."

Hines buildings have won numerous awards from the American Institute of Architects and the Urban Land Institute. Right: ULI's Distinguished Developer Award.

Having the right resources also enables the company to pull off what small local development companies or more centrally controlled national firms often cannot. Hines' regional offices thoughout the United States and overseas enjoy a high degree of autonomy; decisions are made at the local level. At the same time, the firm has a series of central resources that the regions and project managers can call upon. The result is that Hines has the flexibility and maneuverability of a local entrepreneurial firm, while also retaining top-of-the-industry resources.

QUALITY ARCHITECTURE

Quality has been the watchword for Hines from the start. "We operate at the upper end of the quality spectrum in everything we do," Jeff Hines says. "I think Dad was pretty important in bringing that forward as a viable development strategy. He was able to find tenants who were willing to pay for the extra quality. And in down markets, tenants tend to move from Class B and Class C buildings to Class A buildings. So that's where the quality really pays off in reducing your risk during weak office markets."

In the mid-1970s when Hines started building high-rises, Gerald Hines was one of the very first developers to bring in high-profile architects. Prior to that, architects like Philip Johnson had generally been designing homes and civic buildings, not commercial office buildings. Johnson's designs in particular recast corporate architecture in postmodern terms, breaking from the tradition of modernist glass boxes that architect Ludwig Mies van der Rohe had introduced.

The JPMorgan Chase Tower in Houston, designed by I. M. Pei and completed in 1982, is another example of a skyscraper— its slim form has five sides. The seventy-five-story structure was (and remains) Texas' tallest building, the tallest granite-clad building in the world, and the tallest composite concrete and steel building. However, as tall as it is, it is still mindful of the public realm: the tower was placed on one corner of the site to leave the rest of the block free for a large public plaza, providing breathing space for the city.

Hines has worked with many other world-class architects, including Robert A. M. Stern; Frank O. Gehry; Kohn Pedersen Fox; and Skidmore, Owings & Merrill. Many of Hines' projects have garnered awards and accolades for their architectural significance from institutions such as the American Institute of Architects and the Urban Land Institute. Hines buildings have won six awards from the AIA and four ULI Awards for Excellence.

In addition to the large-scale innovation of the company's architecture, however, Hines also introduced innovations on a much smaller scale, bringing in quality features that, as Jeff Hines puts it, "may

not sound terribly noteworthy now, but they were not being done in the marketplace then." They include full-height, nine-foot-high doors, rather than the standard eight-foot doors of the time. From an aesthetic standpoint, full-height doors produce a much cleaner line, eliminating the need to include a transom to fill the space between the top of the door and the ceiling. Hines also introduced high-quality lever door handles to replace the conventional round doorknobs. Today, full-height doors and lever hardware are considered the standard in Class A buildings. For Hines, the attention to detail and the desire to create a quality environment for tenants is as present in a simple piece of hardware used every day as it is in a stunning, angled glass atrium.

Hines' devotion to design innovations extends from the geometry of a skyscraper to the smallest detail, such as full-height, nine-foot doors, right, and high-quality lever door handles, above. Hines introduced both, and like many of the developer's novel ideas, they have become standard in Class A office buildings.

The 1.1 million-square-foot Union Pacific Center in Omaha, Nebraska, opened in 2004. Hines served as development manager for the project. The structure features a dramatic, nineteen-story central atrium, which floods the interior with natural light. The building is designed so that workspaces situated along the building's interior will receive as much natural light as those located along the building's exterior, saving energy.

CONCEPTUAL CONSTRUCTION

One of the most distinctive central resources is the Conceptual Construction group, which is responsible for preconstruction services. For budgeting, design, and contract negotiations, the group brings together all the knowledge Hines has accumulated over the years. "We can learn from our experiences and ensure we don't make the same mistakes in future projects," says Jerrold Lea, senior vice president of Conceptual Construction. "I don't know of another developer that has a group like this—a group that has seen the number of projects that we have seen and that can take all of that knowledge forward."

The roots of the group go back more than thirty years. "In the 1960s, I was supervising the design and construction process for Hines," recalls John Harris, who formed Hines' Conceptual Construction group. "Typically I was involved halfway through construction. Then, as we expanded and were doing One Shell Square in New Orleans, Gerald Hines said, 'It's a waste of your time to be involved in the construction process. Focus on the design and the contracting, and we'll get others to be responsible for the construction process.'"

As Hines established regional offices around the country, each office set up its own construction group. But Hines recognized that it was useful to provide these offices with access to the expertise that had developed over the years. More people got involved in that central function, which expanded from one man to a group of eleven people today. "We're a very independent group," Harris says. "We're responsible for maintaining the Hines emphasis on quality. We feel we're working for the regions. It's a tremendous basis of experience—we've seen any problem that comes up at least twenty times before, and know what to do to resolve it." In addition to Harris and Lea, the team includes a mechanical and an electrical engineer and vice presidents who serve as project leaders.

The Conceptual Construction group is involved in the design of most projects and works with project teams to manage the consultants for that project. It negotiates the consultant agreements and manages their designs as the project goes forward. Over the decades, the Conceptual Construction group has developed a great degree of familiarity with a wide range of consultants. "They know us, they know what we expect, and it gives them a certain comfort level, so the consultants enjoy working with us," says Lea. "The same kind of thing is true with contractors."

At the beginning of the design process, after the building program has been defined, the Conceptual Construction group sits down with the consultants and starts the schematic design process by examining all the alternatives for every building system. The process includes reviewing what competing developers in the area are doing. "We ask ourselves, 'What do our tenants want? What are we going to be able to market effectively?

How do we want to be different from our competition?'" says Lea. The division works with the design team to determine the criteria it will use to compare alternatives for each system. These criteria include first costs, life cycle costs, space usage issues, future flexibility, indoor air quality, life safety issues, and sustainability. Each of those alternatives is evaluated against the overall goals for the building.

The benefit is that the design team starts the project knowing what decisions have been made and why, which enables the team to move forward quickly. In typical development projects, a design team works for a while, the project is priced out and value engineered, and the drawings are then altered to reflect the value engineering. "That's a two-step-forward, one-step-back process," Lea says. "We don't do that. We go through all that analysis at the beginning of the job, so we can tell the consultants, 'Here is what we want, we've tested it against the marketplace, we tested it against our budget, and this is the direction we want to go.'

"And at the end of the process," Lea adds, "we know exactly where we are in comparison to our competition on a system-by-system basis, so we have a great marketing tool. We can go to our tenants and say, 'This is what we're doing and what these other guys aren't, and this is the value it gives you, and this is the analysis we went through that shows you what that value is.'"

As the consultant team is working on schematic drawings, the Conceptual Construction group reviews them for errors and omissions, lack of coordination, and possibilities for more economical or higher quality solutions. "It's almost like a peer review," Lea says. "And because of that process, we tend to have fewer change orders than our competition."

A construction crew works on the subfloor at Ducat Place III, a Hines Class A office building in Moscow. Hines is a leader in underfloor air distribution systems, which supply conditioned air through a raised floor rather than ceiling ducts. The innovation can enhance indoor air quality, increase occupant comfort, reduce energy use, and provide greater flexibility.

The Conceptual Construction group also works closely with consultants and manufacturers to develop new solutions. An example is the underfloor air distribution system for the Owens Corning World Headquarters in Toledo, Ohio, designed by Cesar Pelli and completed in 1996. Owens Corning asked Hines for a state-of-the-art headquarters building that would provide the best possible indoor air quality as well as the ability to accommodate the company's need for staffing flexibility. In the past, Owens Corning had relocated teams within the building through the costly process of moving workstations, conference rooms, and offices. Having the ability to easily make such changes in-house, without having to call in subcontractors, would offer the company significant cost savings.

Underfloor air distribution systems, which supply conditioned air through a raised floor rather than ceiling ducts, can enhance indoor air quality, increase occupant comfort, reduce energy use, and provide greater flexibility. The method was common in Europe, but in the early 1990s few corporate buildings in the United States made use of it. For the Owens Corning project, Hines had a raised-floor system built and then tested it in the laboratory, using the same curtain wall intended for the headquarters building. Testers simulated outdoor temperatures of -20 degrees and 105 degrees, to make sure that the raised floor could supply adequate heating and cooling to the office space. The Conceptual Construction group worked with the manufacturers of the floor grilles to improve them so that they would trap debris safely and be easier for occupants to adjust. Since then, Hines has equipped a number of its buildings with underfloor air systems—"close to seven or eight million square feet," says Lea, "probably more than anyone else in the country. And we've continued to fine-tune it." A recent innovation has been to add a small fan in each structural column to draw air from near the ceiling, warmed by the heat of the light fixtures, down the column, underneath the floor, and out again through the floor grilles to help heat the occupant zone during the winter months.

Hines also gives feedback to manufacturers, working with manufacturers of air-conditioning equipment to achieve new levels of noise reduction or working with vendors to offer advice on lighting. "If you walk through my group's office here," Lea says, "you'll notice that everybody has different lights in their office. We've been in a program where we'll get different light fixtures, put them in the office, and we'll live under that light fixture for a while so we understand what it's like from the user's standpoint. Is there glare on the work surfaces, or glare on the computer screen? Then we can provide that feedback to the lighting manufacturer." The process also means that the group can pass on to tenants its experiences with products, providing an additional service.

Once the Conceptual Construction group has selected a contractor, the group works with that contractor to bid the balance of the work, individually interviewing each of the major subcontractors and examining their bids in great detail. The group also asks the subcontractors to identify any deficiencies they see in the drawings. "The subcontractors, as they're putting their bids together, always give us good feedback about what was missing or not complete or not coordinated," says Lea. "With that feedback, we can deal with those things while we're still in the competitive bid situation and have them revise their bid accordingly. That way, we take care of all that stuff during the bid phase, while we've still got competition, instead of having a change order later, when it costs a lot of money to delay the project."

The group also asks subconsultants to propose cost-saving ideas. Lea says, "We tell them, 'If you give us an idea that's acceptable, it will be to your advantage because it will lower your price as we compare it to your competition's.' So the whole process of getting involved in the subcontractor bidding is very beneficial to us. We think it allows us to save money, to get the very best system possible with as few errors and omissions as possible, and it allows us to really be in control of how we are spending our money. We don't know of anybody else who does it that way."

The reception building in the Owens Corning World Headquarters complex, designed by Cesar Pelli. The curved roof features bright orange porcelain enamel panels that are penetrated with small clerestory windows.

Pei Cobb Freed &
Partners designed
EDF Tower in Paris
for Hines. An elliptical
floor plate adds to
the drama of the
sweeping lobby.

OPERATIONS AND MANAGEMENT

Construction of a project may take several years, but that makes up a small portion of a building's life span. So while selection of quality materials and an emphasis on well-coordinated construction is significant, the ongoing operations have the largest impact on how users experience a building. How comfortable is it to work there? Is the air the right temperature? What if the heating system breaks down in the middle of winter? Is the lighting sufficient for a variety of tasks without causing glare?

Gerald Hines' background as a mechanical engineer gave him unique insight into the value of often-overlooked aspects of successful buildings. "He recognized early on that the operations and maintenance teams were underleveraged and underutilized in the development world," says Clayton Ulrich, vice president and director of corporate engineering services for Hines. "At one point in

time, operations and maintenance were perceived as necessary evils. Through the leadership and innovation of Hines, that's been turned into a core strength. Now the operations, maintenance, and engineering of office buildings are career tracks in a way they never were before, rather than stepping stones to something else." Hines has recognized that by promoting regional engineering managers to officers within the company. "That sets us apart from our competitors," Ulrich adds.

As of 2006, Hines was managing more than one hundred million square feet of property, which gives it a vast pool of experience. To make sure that lessons learned in operations and engineering are taken into account on the front end, an operations engineering/conceptual construction liaison group meets once a quarter to discuss challenges and opportunities on the operations side so that new projects can benefit. And when Hines markets a new development to potential tenants, key operations and building engineering staff are often involved in the presentation to represent the full diversity of Hines' skills. During the design process for a specific project, the Conceptual Construction group also sends drawings to the operations group for review to identify potential cost-saving measures or ways to enhance operations.

Hines also pays an unusual amount of attention to providing quality care to the mechanical equipment in its buildings. Equipment in Hines buildings usually substantially outlasts the normal life cycles listed in the accompanying technical manuals. A good example is at One Shell

As Hines developed a portfolio of world-class structures, it also developed a sophisticated preventive maintenance program to protect its assets. Today, third-party clients benefit from the program in three critical ways: no premature capital expenses, optimal energy management, and minimal unplanned shutdowns.

Plaza, one of Hines' first high-rise towers, completed in 1971. According to Ulrich, "Mr. Hines bought quality equipment when he built the building, and the centrifugal chillers for the air conditioning system are still in place today. And that equipment is operating today at the same level of production efficiency as it did when it was brand new." Hines field-tests major water chilling units regularly to make certain that they are operating at 100 percent of their designed efficiency. That saves significantly on replacement costs.

"We spend an enormous amount of time making sure that we have people who have drive and an interest in customer service," says Tom Kruggel, vice president of operations for the West regional office in San Francisco. "Then we have programs to train people and ways to benchmark how well we are doing."

Hines has also set up several ways to encourage high performance. "We conduct

tenant surveys," Kruggel says. "Jeff Hines himself asks all tenants to fill out the survey. We have a high response rate of 70 to 80 percent, and we benchmark the feedback against information from previous years and against other Hines buildings." There are also internal financial audits, operational audits, and engineering audits. As a result, operations and engineering staffs can compare the energy performance and other aspects of their buildings to those of other Hines properties.

Corporate engineering services functions as a central communication hub for information. In addition, Hines has a best practices program that invites operations and engineering staff to submit ideas that they think other properties would benefit from. A committee evaluates proposals and votes on their applicability, value, innovation, and creativity. The whole company can access the database of best practices, and a recognition program honors those whose ideas are selected.

Corporate engineering services serves as a central communication hub for information. Hines has a program that invites engineers to submit best practices that might benefit other properties. A committee evaluates the proposal, and the best ideas go into a database that can be accessed by everyone in the company.

FINANCING INNOVATIONS

Hines has also been a pioneer in developing new methods of financing projects. Equity-based financing–the practice of raising capital for a development project by selling some percentage of ownership in the building to outside entities–is one of Hines' biggest innovations, breaking away from the standard practice of relying largely on borrowed money.

Initially, when Gerald Hines began as a developer in the 1950s, he raised money for projects the same way as other developers: "At that time, most developers aimed to contribute as little money as they could and borrow as much as they could," says C. Hastings Johnson, executive vice president and chief financial officer for Hines. "The way that the mortgage market worked back then is that for every $100 a project cost to build, you would get an initial loan for, say, $80. As the agent leased the space, the lender would give developers additional advances, so that you could end up borrowing 100 percent of the project cost. Lenders would do this because for every $100 spent on the project, by the time the building was finished, that portion would be worth $120 if it was fully leased. Therefore the lender would only be lending about 80 percent of the value."

Then in the late 1960s and early 1970s, Gerald Hines began developing larger projects, such as the Galleria and One Shell Plaza in downtown Houston. Because of their size, he brought in local business

leaders as equity partners to help reduce the amount of debt.

Hines' big financing revolution came in the early 1970s, when inflation began to soar. At that time, extremely high interest rate loans were common, and Houston was heading into an economic downturn. Hines and Perry Waughtal, former chief financial officer of the firm, started talking about financing with the head of real estate at Shell, who also worked with Shell's pension fund. These conversations led to others with a number of European financing sources about using equity instead of debt to raise money to build projects. In 1974, Hines made a deal with Deutsche Bank to buy a 50 percent equity interest in One Shell Plaza and Two Shell Plaza and a 74 percent interest in Pennzoil Place. These projects were already underway. It wasn't until the late 1970s that Hines first sold equity ahead of time in order to develop a project–for Three First National Plaza in Chicago. The equity partner was the Royal Dutch Shell Pension Fund.

The advantage of equity-based financing is that it removes the initial pressure of having to meet the debt service and provides more flexibility in leasing. Almost all of Hines' projects from the late 1970s through the 1980s were built with equity, most of it offshore equity with entities such as the Deutsche Bank, the Royal Dutch Shell Pension Fund, Nippon Life Insurance Company, and the Kuwaiti Investment Office. Insurance companies in the United States–the dominant sources of debt financing at the time–still preferred to work with debt.

Of course, financing projects with equity instead of debt meant giving up a portion of ownership. Developing with debt requires paying off the loan principal and interest, but once that is done, the developer owns 100 percent of the building. In its equity-financed projects, Hines would end up owning only about 20 to 40 percent of the building. While a conservative way to finance, it was a method that allowed Hines to move from being a local company to becoming a nationwide company. Relying on equity-based financing proved particularly beneficial in the early 1990s when the recession struck. Instead of having to meet debt service on high-interest loans like many developers, Hines and his equity partners were able to hold properties until markets improved.

MARKETING INNOVATIONS

Of course, financing, designing, and building an innovative structure won't do anyone much good if no one is aware of the benefits those innovations bring. When Gerald Hines began hiring prominent architects to create daring designs for speculative office buildings, he had to come up with equally audacious ways to communicate to potential tenants the value of leasing space in these structures.

"We hired nationally known architects to come up with exciting designs, which were more expensive to produce, so it was marketing's responsibility to communicate how leasing in such buildings would enhance a tenant's image," says Pat Harris, former vice president of corporate communications for Hines. "If they leased space in our project, they would be represented by a landmark building for thirty or forty years. With every building we did, our idea was to develop a personality for that building. It had to stand alone, not borrow glamour from some other building."

Before the 1970s, developers relied largely on brochures to market speculative office buildings to prospective tenants. But when Gerald Hines hired Philip Johnson and John Burgee to design Pennzoil Place in the early 1970s, he wanted to create a more powerful experience of what inhabiting the space would be like. Pennzoil Place featured two trapezoid-shaped glass towers connected by a dramatic 115-foot-tall atrium. One of the challenges was to convey to potential tenants what it would be like to walk into such an exciting space. So Hines developed its first marketing center, which occupied a floor in One Shell Plaza. Here, the company displayed a thirteen-foot-high glass model of the Pennzoil atrium—so large that potential tenants could peer inside it.

The marketing center also featured a full-sized mockup of a typical office, completely furnished with desks, chairs, and paintings on the walls. Potential tenants could walk right in and sit down, vividly experiencing what it would be like to work

in the finished product. "We even used the same glass, the same mullions as would be in the final product," Harris recalls. "It was 'marketing vérité.'"

Every major project Hines built thereafter had its own marketing center, which was often used for years, even after the building was completed, because it was so useful in explaining the architecture, it came in handy for re-leasing space. For the Dallas Galleria, completed in 1982, the marketing center featured two walk-in models showing the barrel-vaulted ceilings and features such as the ice rinks. "After a few years, other developers began to build marketing centers of sorts for their projects, but I never heard of one as detailed and thorough as those we created," says Harris.

Audiovisual presentations were also part of the marketing centers. But Gerald Hines didn't want to have a typical slide

When it built Pennzoil Place in Houston in the 1970s, Hines wanted potential tenants to understand the unique quality of the architecture. So Hines developed its first marketing center, which occupied a floor in One Shell Plaza, left. Hines was also known for creative keepsakes, such as the golden shovel, opposite, given to attendees at the groundbreaking of One Shell Plaza.

show or ordinary print collateral. Instead, the company created a ten- to twelve-minute film about each project, complete with voiceover and original soundtrack, and broadcast it on a bank of monitors, which could show separate images or collectively display one large image. The film usually involved an interview with the architect talking about the design. "We concentrated on the architectural experience because we felt that–particularly in the early years–there hadn't been as much striking architecture in Houston as in other cities," Harris says. "It was an untold story. So if we could tell that untold story, people would understand why they might want to spend more money to lease a building with a prominent design."

The creativity extended even to the invitations Hines sent out when announcing a new project. These invitations went out to prospective tenants, the financial community, the city government community, opinion-makers, and the press, encouraging them to come to an event unveiling the new design. For one building, the invitation took the form of a music stand, complete with a

score that bore the wording of the invitation instead of musical notes. For Pennzoil Place, the invitation was a suede notebook with an image of the building on the cover.

Such ingenuity drew the curious. "It wasn't unusual to have 1,500 to 1,800 people at an announcement," Harris recalls. The announcement presentation for Transco Tower (now Williams Tower) in the early 1980s was held at a country club in Houston. While Gerald Hines spoke from the stage, the model of the building slowly rose up through a trap door.

For subsequent marketing centers, Hines would find a floor in an existing building (almost always one that was owned by Hines) overlooking the site of the new building. After the audiovisual presentation had finished, the lights would come up and one of the solid walls in the screening room would slide open to reveal the glass window wall, as the narrator invited guests to walk over and look down at the building under construction.

By enabling prospective tenants to get a strong feel for the quality of the architecture and the materials, it became much easier for tenants to take that leap

At right, the on-site preview center for Park Avenue condominiums in Beijing. The marketing center includes a theater presentation, models, and a furnished unit.

of faith and sign a lease earlier than they might have otherwise. "If you can get one or two big tenants to sign up a few months earlier, then the marketing has paid for itself already," Gerald Hines says. "Since then, a lot of people have started to do the same thing, but we were one of the very first, if not the first, to use that methodology. And it was very, very effective."

INNOVATIONS OVERSEAS

Hines brought its innovative approach to its work overseas as well. As in the United States, the individual offices were given an unusual degree of independence. "Originally, when we began expanding into Europe and opening offices there, we

thought the staff would be made up of 50 percent expatriates from the United States, 50 percent local people," says John Harris. "But as the overseas offices developed, it turned out the locals were very effective. So now our offices in countries like Spain, Germany, and France are 100 percent local." Even in China, where the rapid expansion of the economy has been challenged by a lack of experience in large-scale development, the Hines office now has only ten expatriates in a staff of 260, according to Jim Morrison, Hines' senior vice president in charge of China.

Embassy House, a thirty-two-story, 174-unit luxury high-rise apartment building in Beijing's Second Embassy District, was the company's first project in China. It was

designed to provide high-quality, Western-style living for international businesspeople and the diplomatic community. The project includes a resort-style swimming pool and spa, massage services, hot tubs, a putting green, basketball courts, a billiards room, a café, a fitness center, a library, and a bar—a degree of amenities not uncommon in the West, but rare in China. To build it required a great deal of ingenuity. "It was an enormous challenge to bring Western construction quality to China," explains Jim Buie, executive vice president of Hines' Western U.S. and Asia Pacific regional office. "We had to remake our process

A model of the Cannon Street Underground Station, London. In July 2002, Hines acquired a long leasehold interest in London's Cannon Centre from Marylebone Warwick Balfour Group. Two office buildings totaling 140,000 square feet, originally constructed in the 1960s, are being demolished and replaced by Cannon Street, a new eight-story Class A office development. Through a joint venture with Network Rail, operator of the United Kingdom's railway system, Hines will also renovate the Cannon Street Rail Station.

CANNON STREET UNDERGROUND STATION

of managing on-site work to ensure that the contractors and subcontractors met our expectations. In the late 1990s, the Chinese construction market was still in the early stages of understanding Western standards of quality. This was exacerbated by Hong Kong–based developers who were building many projects in China with low-end standards. Our concept of high end was significantly higher than contractors there were used to. But we found the Chinese contractors very receptive to learning and meeting our expectations." The solution was to place an unusually large number of Hines staff members on-site during construction. Construction lasted for twenty-four months, with around fifteen to twenty Hines employees in the field at all times working with contractors. "If the construction was not up to our standards, we asked them to rebuild," Buie says. "The project was delivered six months behind schedule because of this, but we met the budget. We couldn't have achieved the quality without that daily hands-on work from Hines."

The project has set new standards for development in Beijing. For example, air quality is notoriously poor in Beijing, and the dry air in winter and high humidity in summer can be uncomfortable. For Embassy House, Hines developed a high-quality air purification system which has made the project highly attractive to tenants. "That has given us an enormous competitive advantage," Morrison says. Hines' next big Beijing project, Park Avenue, a master-planned community of five residential mid- and high-rise condominium buildings, will make use of the same kind of system.

While some Western industrial developers are working on projects in China, Hines is the only developer currently active in the residential market, Buie notes. Hines had the deep resources and the willingness to invest many years in researching the market and figuring out ways to introduce its high quality standards. "The learning curve is enormous," Buie says. "I've been doing this for twelve years. Now there are close to three hundred Hines people in China. So we are poised for exponential growth."

Expanding from a local developer to one with a global reach, Hines has come a long way since the 1950s. But it has not calcified as it has grown large. Primarily that is the result of the people Hines hires. Ulrich notes that the company's employees are unusually invested and empowered in their work. "Their days are so diverse and they get exposed to so many different things that it never gets boring," he says. "Their commitment is there because of the recognition and the freedom." That commitment has allowed the company to carry forward Gerald Hines' drive for innovation—continuing to meet and exceed the expectations of its customers while raising the bar for an entire industry.

Jim Morrison (right), who joined Hines in 1987, with fellow Hines executive Bill Larson in the lobby of Embassy House. Morrison was the project officer responsible for the development of the 174-unit luxury apartment tower in Beijing. He heads the firm's China operations.

9

SENSE O

OF PLACE

Hines reshaped Aspen
Highlands Village,
working with Robert
A. M. Stern to develop
an alpine village at the
base of the mountain.

The outdoor café at Panamérica Park, an office/high-tech center in São Paulo, Brazil, takes advantage of the city's temperate climate and provides respite from the bustle of the world's third largest city.

A Sense of Place
by Robert A. M. Stern

We live in an era in which government has, to a considerable extent, surrendered planning to property developers. While too many developers have as yet failed to realize the responsibilities that go with their newly acquired power, such is not the case with Gerald Hines. Hines' greatest gift is his sense of what cities can be. ▨ Long before I was fortunate enough to be introduced to Gerry Hines and to be able to work with him, I recognized that his approach was virtually unique among developers. I first knew of Hines because of the wonderful skyscrapers he was developing in Houston. The skyscraper holds the clearest claim to being a uniquely American building type, and it is easy to forget today how the skyscraper's devaluation in the 1950s and 1960s communicated diminished confidence in American architecture. Hines and his company made their first and most characteristic contribution to our cities at a time when the iconic potential of the skyscraper had fallen out of favor and when the capacity of high-rise commercial buildings to shape public space, as they once had at Rockefeller Center, had been virtually forgotten. During this time, the typical office building filled up its lot or had some sort of unusable plaza designed more to show off the building than to give back to the people any particular sense of place. But a Hines building was more than that, and it was Gerry Hines who kicked off the striking new generation of skyscrapers in American cities. By the early 1970s, New York's status as America's prototypical skyscraper city seemed threatened by the exploding skyline of Houston, Texas.

Pennzoil Place's concourse from the top and the bottom. The twin trapezoidal towers sport distinctive forty-five-degree angles at their crowns. The daring shapes are echoed at the ground level with eight-story glass-enclosed courtyards.

Hines' secret for business success has typically been the same as his secret for architectural success: find the best talent possible and challenge the accepted norms. With Hines' Pennzoil Place (1975), Philip Johnson and John Burgee showed Houston that even a seemingly conventional glass-clad tower could rise above anonymity toward the mythopoeic level of the great skyscrapers of the 1920s. Johnson/Burgee's bold design of twin thirty-six-story trapezoidal towers, each sliced off at a forty-five-degree angle at the top, reminded us of the usefulness of a building's silhouette as corporate symbol and place-marker. The result proved to be good architecture and good business, attracting so many tenants that two floors were added to the design when the building was half erected. But the two towers achieved something else just as important. Between them, a daringly shaped glazed space created something that was more than a typical lobby: it was a concourse, a room that, though not technically open to one and all, had the feel of a public place.

For Houstonians driving the freeways that ring the downtown, Pennzoil Place is an abstract sculpture, enlivened by the ever-shifting slot of sky between the two gray-bronze towers. For those who drive into the downtown core and get out of their cars, the interplaying solid and void

bookend the eight-story glass-enclosed courtyards, which are filled with trees and greenery. Pennzoil Place is as identifiable from the sidewalk as it is on the skyline. Though it never has been the tallest element of Houston's skyline, the two Pennzoil towers—both the glass-covered buildings and the space between them—serve as an identifiable and unique marker for the city.

Hines invited Johnson and Burgee back to contribute to Houston's skyline with the uncompromisingly historicist RepublicBank Center (1983), now the Bank of America Center, across the street from Pennzoil. Its red granite skin and superscaled Dutch gables grin with pride beside the cool glass and geometric purity of Pennzoil. Hines, Johnson, and Burgee also collaborated on the sixty-four-story glass-sheathed Transco Tower (now Williams Tower) in the Post Oak district, which adds a superscaled steeple reminiscent of the best 1920s skyscrapers that tower over the suburban "village" below. With its height and iconic clarity, Transco Tower is a real place-maker—but just as important as its presence on the skyline is the great park and apse-like Water Wall created to the south of the tower. After bland boxes threatened to suffocate the Sunbelt in mediocrity, Gerry Hines gave Houston skyscrapers that not only climb to great heights but also assume a prominent position in the skyline. Hines' buildings stand for something: for the corporations that are their principal tenants and for the art of architecture.

In the 1980s, again working with Johnson and Burgee, Hines established new standards for commercial skyscrapers as icons and place-makers. At 101 California in San Francisco, Hines and Johnson created a building that was a smart response to the very prominent but also very tricky intersection of California and Market Streets. The building was a strong marker that gave identity to its site by emphasizing the importance of the intersection, and physically embracing its surroundings. At the base of the building, instead of the usual empty plaza that would have been left over from the building's circular plan, the lower floors were made to hug the street in an interesting way. Hines facilitated the connection of 101 California to its neighborhood with ingenious programming: newsstands, flower stalls, places for people to sit, all kinds of things that make the building part of the daily life of the city—serving not just people who work in it or visit it for business but for all who frequent the neighborhood.

Philip Johnson introduced Gerry to me in the late 1980s. We worked together on a house design for him in Martha's Vineyard that locked into the seaside architecture of New England. Hines appreciated the contextual sensibility—although, coming from Indiana by way of Texas, it was not something he was familiar with. Then Hines trusted me with some bigger projects, most notably Two Twenty Two Berkeley in Boston, which occupied half of the block where Philip Johnson's Five Hundred Boylston was already under construction. Johnson's design had raised

101 California in San Francisco features a seven-story, glass-enclosed lobby at its base and a granite-paved, triangular plaza which contains seasonal flowers, seating, and a fountain. Throughout the year 101 California hosts many events, including a summer concert series on the plaza, holiday performances, and seasonal art exhibitions.

A sketch for Park City, a city-within-a-city near the heart of Moscow. The Hines development management project on a thirty-eight-acre site on the Moskva River will blend commercial and residential buildings.

Five Hundred Boylston in Boston was originally imagined by Philip Johnson as twin buildings, above right. When local residents objected, Hines asked Robert A. M. Stern to propose a different solution for the project's second tower. The result, above, was Two Twenty Two Berkeley (far left).

a considerable, and not positive, reaction among Back Bay residents who objected to its massing and character; they were opposed to the project's full build-out, which would have resulted in an identical second tower. Confronted with community hostility, Gerry asked me to replace Johnson's plan for the second slab with a different solution. Whereas Philip Johnson's Five Hundred Boylston Street referred to McKim, Mead & White's monumental Boston Public Library, Two Twenty Two Berkeley adapts the red-brick vernacular of Beacon Hill, Back Bay, and the South End. Equally important, perhaps more important, its ground- and second-floor plans invite the public to crisscross the site using shop-lined interior passageways that connect to the building's lobby and to a six-story, glass-roofed winter garden on the building's second floor. The garden is surrounded by shops, with a focal fountain and loose furniture that enable it to function as an indoor piazza—a real public benefit, especially during Boston's long, cold winter months. We made a skylighted courtyard in a private office building into a public place that can also be used for community events.

While Gerald Hines' bread-and-butter work in the 1970s and 1980s was as a developer of office buildings, probably his greatest achievement of those years was the Galleria, a large-scale, urban mixed-use complex. It is perhaps easy to forget how innovative the Galleria was in its day. The Galleria was the first enclosed mall that began to take on urban attitudes—it had hotels, office space, and a health club attached to it, so it became a city within a city. With its multiple levels and focal ice rink, the Galleria became a destination in its own right, and thereby a very successful public place. Hines understood that for every three people who like to ice-skate, three hundred like to watch. The Galleria is place-making at its best—a brilliant new addition to the short list of twentieth-century examples.

Hines has a fabulous weakness: he's like someone who picks up stray cats in a storm, nurses them to their potential, and returns them to healthy productivity. In the early 1990s, Gerry took on a stray cat of place-making: the Highlands, the least developed of the four great ski areas in Aspen, Colorado. Hines called me up one day and said he had the opportunity to take over this property, which had great skiing—some would say the best skiing of all the mountains in Aspen—but only slightly more than nothing in the way of facilities. His challenge was to make this place a destination resort within the larger context of Aspen. One thing we didn't want to do was make the Highlands a reproduction or even a specific emulation of Aspen itself, which was a real town that had become a resort. Gerry knew what made Aspen work as a place; it had been his winter and summer retreat for many years.

The Highlands needed to propose a different model, one that could lift the typical collection of condominium apartments and ski-in, ski-out houses out of banality. We discussed at great length what the Highlands might be. Hines went with a group of his colleagues; my project partner, Graham Wyatt; and me on a seven-day tour of ski resorts in Switzerland, France, and Austria. We toured extensively and exhaustively, visiting sometimes one, two, or three resorts a day in both the traditional towns and the post-war resorts such as Zürs and Lech in Austria. We walked around, measuring with our feet the size of squares and streets, the height of stoops, virtually every physical element that contributed to the townscape. We analyzed in detail the relationship of shops to the public realm; in short, we deconstructed the components of these villages in order to figure out how they worked and, when they failed to work, why. We came away with the understanding that in fundamental ways the great ski resorts, like Aspen itself, were not just places for tourists. People actually lived there all year round; they were real towns that had the great advantage of being next

Gerald D. Hines and Robert A. M. Stern ride in the back of an open truck, above, touring ski villages in Switzerland, France, and Austria to gather ideas for their Highlands development in Aspen, Colorado. In Aspen Highlands Village, Stern drew on the American architectural tradition exemplified by Old Faithful Lodge in Yellowstone Park, Timberline Lodge on Mount Hood, and Paradise Lodge on Mount Rainier.

Hines served as development manager for Petco Park, the home ballpark for the San Diego Padres that opened in 2004. The Antoine Predock–designed ballpark serves as the anchor of a redevelopment effort that turned San Diego's underutilized East Village into a vibrant neighborhood that features hotels, offices, restaurants, and condominiums.

The rustic design of Aspen Highlands Village features native stone, logs, and rough clapboards that form solid walls and broad eaves, which protect residents from the robust Colorado sunlight. Restaurants and shops, together with apartments and a Ritz-Carlton Club, are all grouped around a sun-drenched square along a pedestrian street. Parking for 680 cars is tucked below grade.

to a ski slope. This was the essence of their appeal. In some cases the skiing was quite a ways away, with skiers traveling to the slopes, perhaps by funicular, but always returning in the evening to town, where they could see other skiers, dine in local restaurants, and stay in hotels that were intermixed into a wider rhythm of life.

So with those thoughts and many more, we set out to design the Highlands resort. It was a great project, but not a piece of cake. Some of the locals liked the tumble-down facilities just as they were: great skiing but no amenities to speak of. Today, Aspen Highlands Village is a year-round community with facilities for day skiers, restaurants, and shops, together with apartments and a high-end hotel (a Ritz-Carlton Club), all grouped around a sun-drenched square along a pedestrian street. Parking for 680 cars is tucked below grade where it doesn't intrude. This was an expensive project, but Hines held on to his standards—he made all the right moves. The day skiers, vacationers, and homeowners all intermingle on the slopes and in the streets, in the square, in the restaurants, and at the health club. Of course it takes a long time for a new development to become an organic place—it requires lots of tinkering until it begins to develop its own traditions—but I believe Aspen Highlands is on its way. It's another excellent example of Hines' place-making, which he subsequently brought to his resort projects in Carbondale and Winter Park, Colorado, and Whitefish, Montana.

Then once again, in the mid-1990s, Hines took on another stray cat of place-making. He acquired a long-troubled

shopping center site in Barcelona, Spain. The center was located at the end of the extended Avenida Diagonal, a world-renowned street laid out in the nineteenth century that was blocked from the seashore by rail yards and other industrial sites until they were relocated outside the city in the 1980s. In taking on the site for the Diagonal Mar shopping center, Hines also assumed responsibility for the master planning of a much larger site that included a brand-new park and some sophisticated high-rise housing.

Two previous attempts to build an American-style mall on the site with covered passageways and multiple levels that were crisscrossed with escalators had failed. Hines took it on, challenging our firm with the request that the new mall be streetscape-friendly and that it incorporate a significant outdoor public space—a great square that would serve not only shoppers but the new community as a whole. Instead of building an introspective, American-style mall, Hines understood that the area was now urbanizing and that people, in the Barcelona tradition, would be out walking on the sidewalks.

We successfully reorganized the plan as Hines rewrote lease agreements so that the shops faced the city streets with storefront windows and even second entrances: now activity turns outward and inward at the same time. Taking advantage of Barcelona's year-round gentle climate, we carved a semicircular space out of the triangular lot and lined it with restaurants that opened out to it rather than into the mall. Programming the space with changing activities, Hines succeeded once again in making a convincing public place. Its success makes it a strong identifiable place

In developing the retail mall at Diagonal Mar in Barcelona, Hines wanted a streetscape-friendly development that included significant outdoor public space to serve not only shoppers but the whole community.

A panorama of Diagonal Mar in Barcelona. The design responds gracefully to the center's location overlooking the Mediterranean, with a 54,000-square-foot elevated terrace providing a grand setting for the center's restaurants, bars, and cafés, and a place for patrons to pause and enjoy the view and the sea air. From the outside, the center's glass dome and extravagantly windowed façade glow in the evening light.

within the quarter of culture, residence, and recreation in Barcelona.

Gerry Hines is a developer, but he is also a man who enjoys places. He bicycles, he motorcycles, he walks. He has become increasingly, year by year, impressed with cities; most recently he has pressed for his master plan Porta Nuova to have as much engagement with the city of Milan as possible. The site, which has perplexed the city and other developers since being bombed at the end of World War II, is a great wasteland in the middle of a vibrant city. Here, Hines adds to the usual combination of uses—hotels and office buildings—a large park that organizes the site. On one side the park faces an existing and quite lively neighborhood with restaurants and evening entertainment, theaters, and so forth. On the other side, a street connects the park to the Garibaldi railroad station.

The project brings to Milan American development know-how—the ability to achieve a large project with multiple uses, multiple levels, and complicated infrastructure issues—but it also brings Hines' unique sensitivity to the public realm, a sensibility that is rather European in nature.

Place-making is now second nature for Hines; he goes about shaping the public realm in the same way he goes about every other thing he tackles. He identifies the issues, goes to the right people, grills them about how they view the issue and what kind of solutions they might imagine, and then, with his amazing capacity to translate theoretical or abstract ideas into practical solutions, he makes them happen. His greatest gift is his sense of what cities can be—and then making them that way.

Children feed the swans on the lakefront at Barcelona's Diagonal Mar. Central to the project is a thirty-five-acre public park featuring three lakes, pedestrian walkways shaded by twelve-foot-high pergolas, bicycle and skating paths, three children's play areas, a dog walk area, and multiple water features. The park is the third largest in the city.

THE MAN
THE HISTORY
THE APPROACH
THE LEGACY

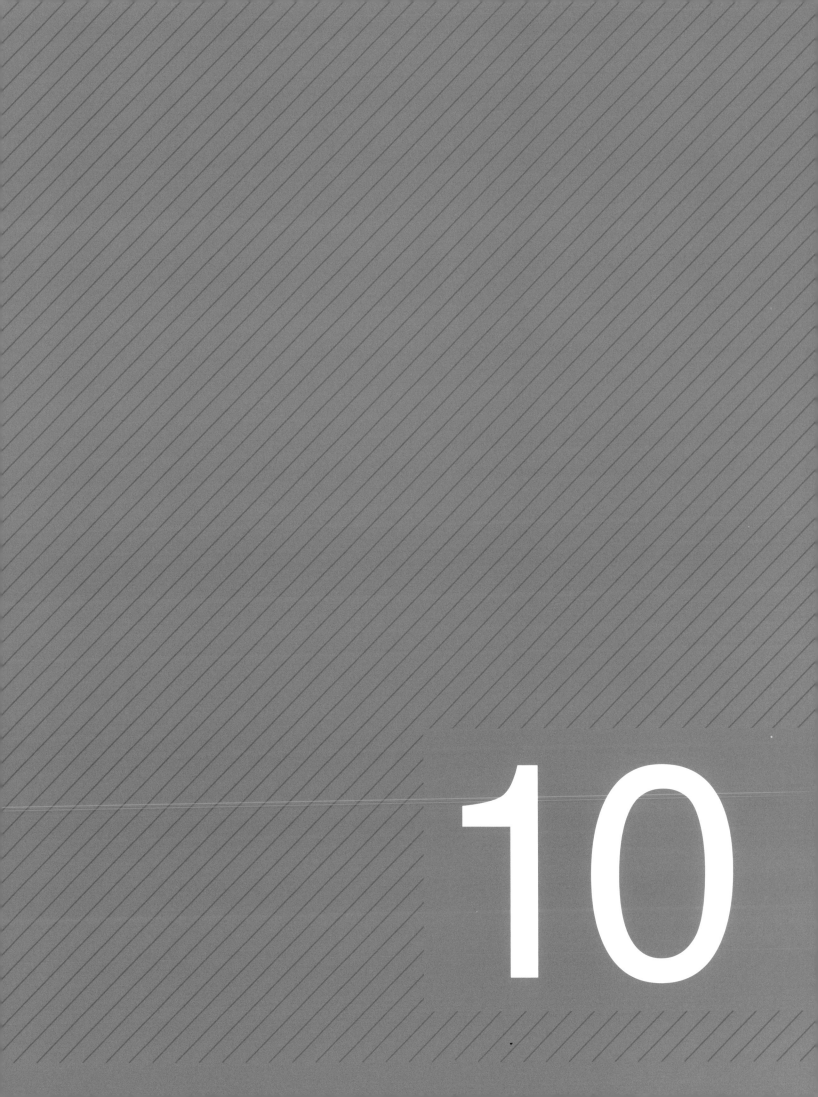

10

The Hines Barcelona
office is attached to a
structure that supports
a vegetated roof. A
green roof is a layer
of living vegetation
that is installed on the
top of a conventional
flat or sloping roof.
It conserves energy
by moderating the
temperature on the
roof and surrounding
areas. It also reduces
storm runoff volume
and peak flow, restores
the ecological and
aesthetic value of
urban open space, and
protects conventional
roofing systems.

SUSTAINABILITY

Sustainability: Leading the Way
by William McDonough

When Ken Hubbard traveled to Texas in 1974 to meet his new boss, Gerald Hines, "green buildings" were just a glimmer in the eye of a few visionary architects. Yet there in petroleum-rich Midland, atop the largest oil field in the United States, Hines was developing an office building notable for how little energy it used. The building, and the vision behind it, made a distinct impression on the thirty-two-year-old Hubbard, now an executive vice president in Hines' U.S. East regional office in New York City and one of the company's leading proponents of sustainable design and green development. ▧ "I'd love to tell you it was one of us that brought sustainability to the firm," Hubbard says. "But that's just how Gerry approached all of his projects as Hines tried to develop the highest quality, most cost-effective building in the marketplace. There were sustainable features in Hines' buildings right from the very beginning." ▧ Fast forward from Midland, Texas, in 1974 to twenty-first-century Washington, D.C., and one finds Hines developing a groundbreaking, four-and-a-half-block, mixed-use downtown neighborhood designed to revitalize an urban community. In most developers' hands, the new neighborhood would likely meet the conventional codes and guidelines set forth by the city, which make only one reference to sustainability. For Hines, however, the project is seen as an opportunity to set a bold, new standard for green development and find better ways to make environmental quality an integral part of urban design.

My own design firm, in fact, is working closely with Hines and the architecture firms Foster and Partners, and Shalom Baranes Associates to develop a sustainable design strategy for the Washington, D.C., site and identify every opportunity to enhance the new neighborhood's environmental performance.

Looking carefully at each aspect of the development, from the technical details of building skins and energy systems to the natural laws that determine the most beneficial orientation to the sun, we ask, "How can we do this better than anyone has done before? How can we continually improve energy effectiveness and indoor air quality and environmental health? How can we make this a vibrant, prosperous place for generations to come?"

Why go to such trouble when much less would do? Because Gerry Hines insists on it. Because the pursuit of quality through sustainable design is not about the maintenance of the status quo but the accrual, over an extended period of time, of the positive benefits of innovation and constant improvement. As Christine Ervin,

former president and CEO of the U.S. Green Building Council, says, Hines is unmatched at making "long-term quality investments while also grasping the potency of emerging trends." Ultimately that's why the company has become synonymous with visionary leadership: vision and constant improvement are a matter of course for the firm, as consistent and deeply ingrained as instinct.

Consider Hines' Conceptual Construction group. Conceived by Gerald Hines in the early 1980s, the Conceptual Construction group is a team of senior engineers who, as team leader Jerry Lea says, "capture the lessons learned from every project and take them forward into the next."

The learning process is not left to chance. Indeed, Lea's Conceptual Construction team guides the Hines design process right from the start, from selecting architects, manufacturers, and general contractors to reviewing the details of architectural drawings and testing new products and building systems. The process is thorough, hands-on, and positive. Open inquiry is highly valued, and every choice, every design decision, is seen as an opportunity to enhance environmental quality. "We never rest," says Lea. "We are constantly trying to improve on what we've done."

As a result, the Conceptual Construction team is always a step ahead, pushing hard for innovation. Once they've defined a project's design strategy and selected what appear to be the most effective green technologies available, the group measures its decisions against the leading buildings and practices in

Ken Hubbard, executive vice president of Hines' U.S. East regional office in New York City, around the time he joined Hines in 1974. He is one of the company's leading proponents of sustainable design and green development.

When Hines broke ground on One South Dearborn in Chicago, right, its goal was to create a building that promoted heath and productivity for tenants. The result is a forty-story metal and glass tower with such amenities as an outdoor plaza and on-site fitness center. The property received LEED Silver designation from the U.S. Green Building Council in 2006.

When I. M. Pei designed Columbia Square in the mid-1980s, few builders were thinking green. The development foreshadowed the sustainability movement with its highly efficient energy systems. For example, at favorable outside air temperatures, the building is able to operate in the economize mode using plate-to-plate heat exchangers. It also incorporates mass transit, with Metro access beneath the building.

the marketplace. If a competitor is doing something notable, they revisit a decision and explore new solutions. The goal, always, is to be "best-in-class" in every aspect of sustainable building design.

"We challenge our consultants to make us think beyond our last building," explains Hubbard. "Don't just look at what we last built. Tell us what we should be building next."

As each "next building" is completed, Lea's group circles back and reviews the project in great detail, gathering information from Hines' construction and operations managers, assessing the performance of contractors, and evaluating the effectiveness of their own design decision-making. Through teamwork and information-sharing, knowledge evolves, and, project by project, bold innovations become standard practice.

For years Hines' conceptual construction process yielded "best-in-city" developments all over the country. In Washington, D.C., for example, even Hines' competitors agreed that I. M. Pei's Columbia Square set a new standard for commercial office buildings when it was completed in 1987. No one then was talking about sustainability, but Columbia Square presaged the movement with its cutting-edge, highly efficient energy systems and its contribution to urban density and effective mass transit; with Metro subway access located directly beneath the building, Columbia Square became a vibrant community hub.

By the early 1990s Hines' culture of constant improvement was increasingly equating quality with strong environmental performance. The company was so adept at responding to environmental concerns it created its own indoor air quality guidelines in 1992, before either the Environmental Protection Agency or the U.S. Green Building Council (USGBC) had developed their own. In fact, says Lea, Hines invited the EPA into the process, getting referrals for trusted experts in the field to "make sure we were doing the right thing." As it turned out, Hines' original indoor air quality guidelines—which call for ventilating buildings during construction, selecting healthful, non-toxic materials, providing natural ventilation, and circulating abundant fresh air—are very much in tune with the requirements developers now try to meet to earn credits in the USGBC's Leadership in Energy and Environmental Design (LEED) rating system for green buildings.

After developing its robust indoor air quality standards, Hines didn't simply resort to "catalogue engineering" to meet them. Instead, the firm developed new, even more effective ways to supply clean, fresh air to the occupants of their buildings. At the JPMorgan Chase Building in San Francisco, a thirty-one-story tower designed by Pelli Clark Pelli, the ventilation system uses 100 percent outside air. In conventional office buildings, which typically recirculate indoor air, only about one third of the ventilated air comes from outside. At 600 Thirteenth Street, a commercial development in Washington, D.C., Hines installed an electronic air filtering system that virtually eliminates the circulation of dust and other fine particles. At 50 South Sixth Street in Minneapolis,

In 2004, Hines acquired 101 Second Street in San Francisco, above, through its U.S. Office Core Fund. Hines was able, through improved operating efficiency, to garner an Energy Star designation from the EPA for the property. The building's four-story, glass-clad atrium serves as an art pavilion while its street-level glass panels can be opened on warm days to bring the outdoors in.

At the JPMorgan Chase Building in San Francisco, a thirty-one-story tower designed by Pelli Clark Pelli, the ventilation system uses 100 percent outside air. In conventional office buildings, which typically recirculate indoor air, only about one third of the ventilated air comes from outside. The floor-to-ceiling glass and column-free space throughout the building allow for 360-degree access to light and air.

Hines engineers introduced an ultraviolet light system that further treats and cleanses the indoor air stream. Now, 100 percent fresh air delivery, electrostatic filters, and UVC cleaners are considered for every Hines building, often in tandem.

These innovations are not simply technological advances; they're about enhancing the environment and the experience of every Hines building. Lea recalls how the tenants at 600 Thirteenth Street responded to the apparently rare good fortune of breathing exceedingly fresh air. "'We don't know what it is about this building,' they kept telling the building managers, 'but we just feel better here.'"

Clean air is not the only accruing benefit of Hines' culture of constant improvement; there are also best practices that value clean water, a stable atmosphere, abundant energy, healthy landscapes, and prosperous communities—the fundamental qualities of a sustainable world. And, as with the air quality standards, these other sustainability benchmarks have evolved not from external pressure or admonition but out of a deep well of rigorous idealism that is as precise and sensible as it is inspiring.

One sees the results in every project. Consider the way water is valued at 1180 Peachtree, Hines' forty-one-story skyscraper in Atlanta. A high-performance green building, the office tower has a partially vegetated roof that absorbs rainfall and channels storm water to an underground vault, which also captures the condensation from HVAC systems. The pooled water is used to fully irrigate the building's grounds year-round without a single drop of city water. Factoring in annual rainfall and runoff, engineers designed the vault so that it will never run dry.

In all aspects of design, construction, and maintenance, Hines' engineers strive to optimize quality and environmental

performance. Indeed, superior engineering has always been the rock-solid foundation of every Hines building. High-tech building control and monitoring systems; cutting-edge energy management software; motion sensors for optimum office lighting; and super-efficient transformers, chillers, and ventilation technology all add up to long-term reliability, energy savings, and tenant comfort.

Ultimately it may be Hines' company-wide commitment to excellence that makes the biggest difference. Hines' building operators and property managers are said to be "fanatical" about fine-tuning every system, and it's their constant, reliable feedback that keeps Hines' design teams in tune with how green technologies really work.

Maintenance engineers ensure that building systems are running efficiently at Hyundai Motor Tower in Beijing, above, which is managed by Hines. The twenty-four-story, 600,000-square-foot Class A office building was designed by the late Minoru Yamasaki, the Japanese-American architect who designed the Twin Towers of New York City's World Trade Center.

101 Queen Victoria Street in London, the global headquarters of the Salvation Army, was completed in 2004. Full-height glazing on the building's façade maximizes natural light to offices while a vibrant, six-story atrium houses a public café where staff can interact with visitors. The project received the city of London's top architectural award.

In 1999, Hines entered a partnership with Energy Star, an EPA greenhouse gas reduction program that recognizes commercial buildings for superior energy performance. The rating tool gave Hines independent verification of its internal high standards for energy efficiency. By 2006, more than ninety major office buildings owned or managed by Hines, encompassing fifty-four million square feet, had secured the coveted label. Hines was named Energy Star Partner of the Year for three straight years, and in 2004 became the only real estate company to be honored with the program's Sustained Excellence Award.

"Our commitment to sustainability reaches from top to bottom, to the furthest reaches of the ranks and back," says Jim Green, vice president of engineering. "We could talk all day about what drives we use, what occupancy sensors, what energy management systems, but it's the person who operates or maintains the building that's the real energy manager; the one who goes out and maintains the pump or the fan or the motor and asks every day, 'How is what I'm doing going to impact the energy profile of this building and how can I make it better?' That's just a part of our culture."

In 1999 Hines began measuring the impact of its culture when it entered a partnership with Energy Star, an EPA greenhouse gas reduction program that recognizes commercial buildings for superior energy performance. "The rating tool provided Hines independent verification of the high standards for energy efficiency that the company mandated for itself," says Stuart Brodsky, Energy Star's national program manager. "Often, Hines found that it exceeded those standards, and at times found opportunities for improvement, which it has tirelessly pursued."

Indeed, in 2006 more than ninety major office buildings owned or managed by Hines had secured the coveted label. That's fifty-four million square feet, nearly one quarter of all non-government Energy Star–rated office space in the U.S. For three consecutive years, beginning in 2001, Hines was named Energy Star Partner of the Year, and in 2004, the firm became the only real estate company to be honored with the program's Sustained Excellence Award. A study completed in 2000 found

that Hines buildings in the program were generating a total of $13 million in portfolio-wide savings annually.

Every individual feature of a building that saves energy or cleanses the air or conserves water is valuable. But buildings get really interesting, and deliver marvelous results, when a variety of features are brought together in fully integrated designs—designs that make the whole greater than the sum of its parts and support a wide spectrum of human values.

Hines excels at that, too. Since 2000, Hines senior management has been meeting with my firm, William McDonough + Partners, to explore a range of complex questions about sustainability and green design. We've looked at the cost-effectiveness of renewably powered facilities. We've discussed design protocols that assess the human and ecological health effects of building materials, right down to the parts per billion. We've exchanged dramatic and subtle information on green technologies, health and productivity, and the principles of natural systems. In other words, we're imagining the future.

And it looks like this:

It's 717 Texas, Houston's greenest building, which creates an extraordinarily healthful environment with natural light, safe materials, filtered air and drinking water, and personal climate control—and extends environmental attention all the way to the reusable moving containers Hines used to move into the building.

It's Atlanta's 1180 Peachtree, which, in addition to its vegetated roof that absorbs water and heat, integrates a wide range of features into a high-performance building, including glass cladding that reflects more heat than it absorbs; locally sourced and recycled building materials; super-efficient

Among the sustainable innovations at 717 Texas, a thirty-two-story, Class A office tower in Houston: outside air is electrostatically cleansed through a high-efficiency filtration system to eliminate pollutants. A floor-by-floor air quality monitoring and control system monitors supply and return air, and allows for the adjustment of fresh-air volume to minimize carbon dioxide concentration. Surface treatments, flooring, ceiling tile, and other finish materials were selected based on their use of recycled contents and the low percentage of volatile organic compounds that they contain. 717 Texas' drinking water system delivers filtered, chilled drinking water to every floor, eliminating the need for bottled water delivery.

CALPINE CENTER 717 TEXAS

Atlanta's 1180 Peachtree features a vegetated roof that absorbs water and heat; glass cladding that reflects more heat than it absorbs; locally sourced and recycled building materials; super-efficient low-volume faucets; environmentally safe carpets and adhesives; and bike racks and showers for walking and biking commuters. It was the first high-rise office building in the Southeast to win the coveted LEED Gold certification from the U.S. Green Building Council.

Hines vice president Grant Stevens (left), Gerald Hines, and vice president Mary Hill at 1180 Peachtree. Hines sold the 670,000-square-foot building in 2006, but continues to manage and lease the property.

low-volume faucets; environmentally safe carpets and adhesives; and bike racks and showers for walking and biking commuters. All of this made it the first high-rise office building in the Southeast to win the coveted LEED Gold certification from the U.S. Green Building Council.

It's Diagonal Mar, an eighty-four-acre mixed-use community Hines developed on a former industrial site in Barcelona, a project that extends principles of green building to urban design. At Diagonal Mar buildings are oriented on the solar grid to optimize sunlight in winter and air circulation in summer. All have rainwater collection systems for irrigation and use solar panels to preheat water. Swimming pools are also heated by solar panels and much of the pavement is porous to allow water to flow through and percolate into the soil. Within Diagonal Mar is a thirty-five-acre public park, the third largest in the city. Like 1180 Peachtree, Diagonal

Mar's design set a new standard, winning the first European Award for Excellence from the Urban Land Institute.

Throughout Europe, says Jay Wyper, Hines' London-based senior vice president for development, "we are meeting and exceeding tough environmental regulations and in many cases setting new standards for sustainable design where none existed before." Hines' public-private sustainability agreement with the Municipality of Barcelona was the first of its kind in Europe, as was the LEED certification program it implemented for two new developments in Milan. In Paris, Hines' massive Renault redevelopment seeks to exceed local sustainability standards through a combination of master planning, density with public transit, and green infrastructure in the design of each and every building. This "macro-micro approach," Wyper says, "typifies Hines' large-scale projects in Europe." And the lessons learned on these projects often inform the design of Hines' new projects in the United States;

the standard-setting macro-micro approach to sustainability, for example, can be seen in the comprehensive design strategy for Hines' new urban development in Washington, D.C.

These are all extraordinary achievements. What makes them even more remarkable is the fact that Hines is developing high-performance green buildings for the speculative office market, which demands that every green feature pay off on the bottom line.

"You can't talk about your commitment to sustainability or about broad public policy issues and convince a tenant to sign a lease on a building," says Hubbard. "On the other hand, if we really focus on making the case that our buildings have a competitive advantage because we pay attention to sustainable standards, then we have a winning business strategy as well."

Parc Diagonal Mar resulted in the first-ever public/ private sustainability agreement in Spain, a pact between Hines and Barcelona's town hall, which governed the park design, construction, and operation. The park was designed with porous pavements that minimize storm water runoff; native plants specified to curtail irrigation and pesticide applications; time-controlled fountains and smaller fountains that spray a mist at low pressure; irrigation system water provided from the park's lake; wetland areas around parts of the lake for storm water filtration; and lake bottoms at two meters below the water's surface, allowing groundwater to be the lake's primary source of water.

Franklin Square in Washington, D.C., won an Energy Star award a decade after construction was completed for efficient upgrades. Fluorescent lighting was retrofitted to include electronic ballasts and T-8 fluorescent lamps, and climate-control systems were retrofitted for greater efficiency.

Hines hasn't limited itself to making that point to its clients, however. It has broadcast the business case for high performance green buildings to the entire industry and beyond, creating enormous public value in the process.

"It's one thing to market green," says Christine Ervin, former president and CEO of USGBC, "but it's another to invest the time and the resources and the whole value of your corporation's brand to transform the marketplace."

And that's just what Hines has done. Soon after USGBC launched the LEED Green Building Rating System in 2001, Hines embraced the new standards, giving the fledgling organization solid ground to stand on. "There is always a critical juncture when credibility can make or break you, and for USGBC and LEED, Hines played that linchpin role," says Ervin. "LEED had received a strong market reaction, but if we were ever going to influence the mainstream market, we needed to move very quickly from the niche of true believers to the mainstream innovators. Hines' early, deep, incredible involvement made a big difference for us and allowed us to move more quickly down the path toward market transformation."

Gerald and Jeffrey Hines put the full weight of their influence and organization behind LEED. When USGBC needed to articulate the economic reasons for adopting sustainability standards, Hubbard chaired a task force that developed a ten-point business case for green buildings. Within six months, Ervin recalls, the USGBC had distributed the document to every member of Congress and to thousands of companies as well, while Hubbard took the case directly to the press and later, to the influential Urban Land Institute. Today, the key points the group identified—lower operating costs, better employee productivity, enhanced health, and increased property values—have been widely accepted.

Jerry Lea, meanwhile, volunteered to lead the development of the LEED Core and Shell standards, which gave real estate firms in the speculative market a new set of green guidelines. Lea, in fact, had identified the need for those standards, which had not been included in the original LEED rating system. His involvement, says Ervin, was "an amazing contribution, not only because of his personal skills and leadership, but for the integrity and industry influence that Hines brought to the process."

Hines played a similar role in the EPA's Energy Star program, which helps companies track the financial and environmental advantages of energy efficiency. "As an early adopter of Energy Star tools," explains Brodsky, "Hines provided invaluable feedback to the EPA, thereby making our tools and resources even more accessible to the industry. Because of Hines' reputation as a thought leader in development and management

practices, its early adoption of our program also encouraged the rest of the real estate industry to consider its benefits."

Hines' support for USGBC and Energy Star suggests how deeply the organization is committed to leadership in the industry, and how leadership can only be sustained by the wisdom, heart, and drive of individuals. People like Gerry and Jeff Hines, to be sure, but also Hines people from the furthest reaches of the ranks.

Mike Greene, vice president of design and construction in Hines' Washington, D.C., office, describes the firm's idealism. "It runs all through the company," he says. "We have executives leading the charge but we also have junior people on our staff out getting their LEED certification and studying and asking us, 'Why aren't you trying this or trying that?' On a renovation project in D.C., it was the construction manager pushing everyone to get a higher and higher LEED certification. The leasing guy was saying that the tenant didn't really care, but the construction manager was able to convince everybody that sustainability is a good idea and we should be thinking about it everywhere. Our property managers take air quality

personally. We have inspired engineers who are going to perform miracles because it's in their blood to do that now; they challenge each other to get Energy Star ratings for acquired buildings. Even new employees with no knowledge of architecture or design get caught up in the culture. Sustainability gives us all an opportunity to be idealistic."

One sees the towering legacy of Gerald Hines' idealism, intelligence, and energy in the beautiful buildings and lively urban places, in the values of the Hines culture and dreams of its young designers, in the enduring standards and communities just now emerging.

Reflecting on the Hines legacy, Ken Hubbard sees not only "a movement toward a higher degree of sustainability and a higher degree of performance in green buildings," but a culture poised to carry that sense of purpose far into the future. "What we've done so far," he says, "is only the beginning."

Hines acquired 225 South Sixth, the I. M. Pei–designed, 1.4-million-square-foot office tower in downtown Minneapolis and one of the area's most prestigious properties. Hines oversaw retrofits and upgrades to the building's energy-consuming infrastructure, garnering the Energy Star certification. Hines sold the building in 2006.

ART

11

Rickey Castanis Dubuffet

Moroles Kelly Miró Moore

A Commitment to Art
by Ann Holmes

On a June afternoon in 1972, Gerald Hines, already a major builder in Houston, stepped in front of a large gathering of civic leaders and journalists. In announcing the next project of Gerald D. Hines Interests, Hines had news that would fascinate the crowd and usher in a new architectural era locally, nationally, and internationally. ▪ The developer had commissioned New York architect Philip Johnson and his then-partner John Burgee to design what became an eye-popping new building for Houston, Pennzoil Place. As the architecture critic for the *Houston Chronicle*, I was there and within a few days made an appointment with Hines, whom I had yet to meet. I had congratulations for him, of course, and a few questions. Up close, Mr. Hines was a gentle, smiling businessman. As he seated me comfortably on the sofa, he asked, "What can I do for you, young lady?" ▪ "It's what you can do for the people," I replied–rather cheekily, I now realize. "What might you give back?" ▪ "What would you suggest?" he asked. "A fountain? A sculpture?" ▪ Just as Pennzoil Place would revolutionize architectural styling, Hines would go on to be one of the great quiet patrons of civic art. As the city grew I was able to write of his early burst of activity in Houston and follow him as he provided his adopted hometown with a soaring, brightly colored sculpture by Dubuffet; a felicitous Miró sculpture at the city's tallest building; and a chimerical art piece, the Water Wall at Philip Johnson's Transco (now Williams) Tower.

Across the country, Hines has installed such bold works as a towering bronze sculpture by Henry Moore in Chicago; twelve ghostlike goddesses atop a mansard roof in San Francisco; and a monumental granite sculpture in New York that is one of the most highly praised public works in Manhattan. In Los Angeles, Hines has commissioned waterfalls that collide with fire (calling to mind the French artist Yves Klein and his fountains of fire and water), while in Cincinnati, three-dimensional quilts, ordered by Hines himself, hang like mixed-media sculptures (reminiscent of Robert Rauschenberg's 1955 painting that grows out of a canvas into an unmade bed). Abroad, Hines has created a remarkable public park with bold aluminum sculptures in Barcelona and a sculptural, organic conference room by Frank Gehry floating in a majestic atrium in Berlin.

"I felt art would increase the awareness of buildings in the public marketplace," Hines now explains. "And I thought commissioning and buying art would be enriching for the city and the built environment."

Leading builders have long understood the power of great public art, including John D. Rockefeller and the sculptures he installed at Rockefeller Center as well as the famous Diego Rivera mural deemed too controversial and forcibly removed from the walls. Many corporations have also been clear on the benefits of commissioning art for their headquarters. But few speculative developers seem to have taken the time and trouble that Hines has to make serious artistic statements. "There are some but not many, I guess," the soft-spoken Hines concedes. "Although you have to remember that Rockefeller was a speculative developer—he just had a little deeper pockets than old Gerry Hines."

Hines also wants to make it clear that the artistic efforts put forth by his firm were collaborations. "We have been able to work with people like Ben Love [the late chairman of Texas Commerce Bank] and Jack Bowen [former chairman of Transco], who all felt strongly about art. They really make a city; they feel a sense of responsibility to the built environment. And then we've worked with architects, from Philip Johnson to I. M. Pei, who have a real feel for art. So it's not just the developer—it's also the CEOs, the tenants, the architects."

The first example of Hines' support for public art took place in Cincinnati, with the 1979 completion of PNC Center, a twenty-seven-story white marble and black glass structure designed by Skidmore, Owings & Merrill. Cincinnati has long had a vital arts community, so a local artist was hired to paint watercolors of the city for the marketing brochure. "That set the scene for this project and the theme just continued forward from there," remembers Tom Owens, a Hines senior vice president. "The chairman of the bank, Oliver Burkhead, and Gerry got along great and they really wanted to do some permanent artwork for the building."

The bank, which at that time was the Central Trust Company, commissioned a spectacular work by Ellsworth Kelly, *Color Panels for a Large Wall*, a series of eighteen monochrome canvases that stretched across a 140-foot-long wall above the bank tellers. (The work has since been installed in the National Gallery of Art in Washington.) For the exterior of the

At right, Ellsworth Kelly's *Color Panels for a Large Wall*, a series of eighteen monochrome canvases that stretched across a 140-foot-long wall above the bank tellers in Cincinnati's PNC Center. The work was subsequently installed in the National Gallery of Art in Washington, right.

building, Hines and Burkhead chose kinetic sculptor George Rickey (1907–2002), whose *Two Rectangles Vertical Gyratory II, Variation IV*, is a stunning kinetic sculpture. Rickey's towering piece, in hand-polished stainless steel, features two rectangular panels on top of a twenty-eight-foot-tall shaft that shift and spin in the wind. The panels rotate around a horizontal bar at the same time the bar turns around the vertical shaft. The sculpture is a striking example of the balances and counterbalances that Rickey, playing with the forces of wind and gravity, utilized in his work.

"Both of those artists were up near northern New York at the time," Owens remembers. "I remember going up there with the architect, Rick Keating—then with Skidmore, Owings & Merrill. We went over to Ellsworth Kelly's studio to meet with him and we went up to see George Rickey—we had lunch with him and his wife in their farmhouse. When Rickey came to Cincinnati to install the artwork, he was really interested in making sure that we maintained it. We had our chief engineer create a preventive maintenance schedule."

The following year, 1980, Gerald Hines commissioned his first internationally significant work of art in Houston for 1100 Louisiana, a fifty-five-story pink granite and reflective glass building designed by Skidmore, Owings & Merrill. The structure

is situated on an enormous plaza covering a quarter of a block, which the developer and architect decided would be home to a bold sculpture by legendary French artist Jean Dubuffet (1901–1985). The finished piece, *Monument au Fantôme*, was one in a group of small works being considered for enlargement and sale in American cities, to be placed in prominent public spaces. It was part of a series called *Hourloupe*, a nonsensical term Dubuffet explained as "Some wonderland or grotesque object or creature, the figuration of a world other than our own, or parallel to ours." In 1972, three *Hourloupe* sculptures were created as studies for a commission for the corporate headquarters of the Chase Manhattan Bank of New York. Bank chairman David Rockefeller chose the well-known *Group of Four Trees* for One Chase Manhattan Plaza (also designed by Skidmore, Owings & Merrill). Hines spoke up for *Fantôme* for 1100 Louisiana.

As Gerald Hines remembers, "With Chuck Bassett, the design partner in the San Francisco office of Skidmore, Owings & Merrill, we went to visit Dubuffet at his studio in Paris. He came up with some suggestions and made little maquettes of the works. We moved them around a little bit and looked at the different possibilities. Chuck Basset really helped with that—he had a real feeling about how the sculpture should look in relation to the building."

Monument au Fantôme is a group sculpture of seven individual pieces in vivid red, white, blue, and black. The tallest, at thirty-three feet, is called *Mast*. Other pieces are labeled *Church*, *Trees*, *Phantom*, *Dog*, *Chimney*, and *Hedge*. Dubuffet expert Andreas Franzke, author of several books on the artist, described

Houston's bright *Phantom* as "a small, imaginative townscape—almost like that a child might see in a dream." Decorated with acrylic paints on epoxy resin, the sculptures were created in France, shipped to the Port of Houston, and taken by truck to the building site (where they became a focus of peeking eyes in their neighborhoods as they were assembled). The huddled creatures of *Phantom* are a witty response to the seriousness of the towering business buildings surrounding them, a refreshing change from the disciplined orders of downtown life.

"I think it has stood the test of time," Hines says of the sculpture. "And I think that's what the criteria should be."

The following year, 1981, with the completion of Three First National Plaza in Chicago, Hines unveiled another internationally significant sculpture, by distinguished English artist Henry Moore (1898–1986). The fifty-seven-story tower, designed by Skidmore, Owings & Merrill in pale granite and tinted glass, features a nine-story central atrium. "This was our first major building in Chicago and we wanted to create a good atmosphere there," Hines explains. "We felt that a sculpture in that atrium would be a nice way to contribute to the city."

To organize the commission, Hines went over to Hoglands, a seventeenth-century, timber-framed farmhouse in Hertfordshire, north of London, where Henry Moore lived with his wife, Irina. "We went out to his little house out there in the country," Hines says. "It was so ancient, we had to stoop down to get in the door. His wife was Russian,

and they had a lot of his sculptures behind the house, on the rise of a plane against the sky, which we walked out to see. He was just so down-to-earth—we'd walk through the village, past his neighbor, and he would say, 'Well hello, Mrs. Stafford, how are the chickens doing today?' He was a wonderful person."

The work Moore created for Three First National Plaza, *Large Upright Internal/ External Form*, is truly monumental. It is a large bronze abstract form enveloping a smaller form, with the exterior element encircling and protecting the smaller, enclosed shape. As the Henry Moore Foundation characterizes this series, "The vulnerability of the interior element is emphasized by the strength of the encircling or embracing exterior form." Moore's sculpture, fixed in the entrance of this cathedral of commerce, is like an abstract Madonna and child.

In 1982, Hines and architect I. M. Pei completed the JPMorgan Chase Tower in Houston, a seventy-five-story, one-thousand-foot-high, five-sided structure in pale gray granite, stainless steel, and gray glass. The tallest building outside of New York or Chicago, this slender tower occupies an entire city block. As Pei was well along with the design of his stunning structure, Ben Love, the chairman of Texas Commerce Bank (the building's original tenant), joined the developer and architect in a quest for a major sculpture for the large public space. In a memoir published shortly before his death, *My Life in Texas Commerce*, Ben Love wrote, "Our objective was to enliven street life in downtown Houston and focus national attention on Houston's cultural achievements."

Gerald Hines has taken a hands-on approach to selecting the art for many of his buildings. For Three First National Plaza in Chicago, Hines (arms crossed) visited sculptor Henry Moore in his studio north of London, top, and commissioned a bronze, opposite. At bottom (from right) JPMorgan Chase Tower architect I. M. Pei, tenant Hugh Roff, Hines, and tenant Ben Love meet artist Joan Miró (far left) in Mallorca to review a maquette of *Personage and Birds*.

All involved settled on the renowned Spanish artist Joan Miró (1893–1983). "We had a large plaza, one of the largest ones in Houston, and felt that it was important to put a strong piece of sculpture there," Hines remembers. "So we proceeded to look down different paths and with I. M. Pei, we came up with Miró. His work had a sense of fun. Texas Commerce was a very serious bank—they wanted this piece to have a little whimsy about it."

I. M. Pei first saw a five-foot unpainted cast bronze maquette of the Miró sculpture *Personage and Birds* at the New York gallery of Pierre Matisse. When Pei projected the work in scale, blowing it up nearly eleven times, he felt the piece would need bright color. Miró agreed. Pei, Hines, Love, and Hugh Roff (chairman of United Energy Resources, another major tenant in the building) set off to see the artist. "We went to Majorca to meet with Miró," Hines remembers. "We spent a day there, showing him the plans for the plaza, showing him the drawing of the building. I. M. Pei, who is just a gem in terms of his breadth of knowledge, did most of the talking. Pei speaks the language—he's a very sensitive architect."

Personage and Birds, at the entrance to JPMorgan Chase Tower, is a monumental sculpture in steel and cast bronze that rises to fifty-two-and-one-half feet tall and weighs sixty-one tons. It is the largest Miró

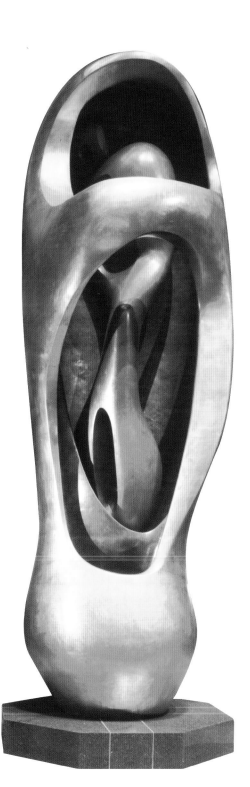

sculpture in America. With its bright shades of green, red, blue, yellow and black, *Personage and Birds* sends a festive tune into the air. It was dedicated on April 20, 1982, the artist's eighty-ninth birthday. At the dedication, Hines told the crowd that the Miró "adds a sense of humanism to the city, since it sits there in front of a serious banker's gray granite building. Frankly, it tickles my funny bone."

Pei's design for the JPMorgan Chase Tower also included a sixtieth floor sky lobby, the highest public observation area in Houston. Displayed in the lobby is the tapestry *Six Flags Over Texas*, a reference to the six national flags that have flown over the state of Texas in its history. It is the work of prominent weaver Helena Hernmarck. A native of Sweden, Hernmarck is based in Ridgefield, Connecticut. Her work, which brings a camera-like realism to thread art, has been featured in the Montreal Expo, Cunard's Queen Elizabeth II, and such important buildings as Atlanta's Bank of America Tower, Boston's World Trade Center West, and New York City's Time Warner Center. Also included in the sky lobby are two Miró sculptures: *Disheveled Woman*, which was also considered for the plaza, and *Personage and Birds*, the original version of the artist's masterpiece that now stands sixty floors below.

The year after the Miró work was unveiled, in 1983, Gerald D. Hines Interests completed another remarkable building in Houston, Transco Tower (now Williams Tower) by Philip Johnson. Surely no one would think the extraordinary structure,

Personage and Birds, at the entrance to JPMorgan Chase Tower in Houston. The sculpture by Joan Miró is constructed of steel and cast bronze, rises to fifty-two-and-one-half feet tall, and weighs sixty-one tons. It is the largest Miró sculpture in America.

Atop Williams Tower, above, is a seven-thousand-watt rotating beacon that makes a 360-degree sweep across the Houston sky every fifteen seconds.

a sixty-four-story, reflective glass jewel, inspired by such art deco masterpieces as the Empire State Building, would need any work of art to be complete. But the tower stands at the northern portion of a three-acre open park and architects Johnson and Burgee couldn't let that opportunity get by. They created a grandiose and exciting folly, a fantastic architectural waterfall-within-a-box. "That was a suggestion of Philip's," says Hines. "Jack Bowen, the CEO of Transco, thought we could create that area to the south of the building, make a little park. And Philip came up with the idea of the water fountain—it's an extraordinary experience."

The Williams Tower Water Wall is a show of its own. A sixty-four-foot-high curved wall of black obsidian sets off the crash of 11,800 gallons of water per minute that finishes on a gently curving ring of steps at the bottom. The cataract comes down the front and the back side

of the giant wall, and the movement of the water, paired with the absence of a view of the horizon line, produces a multisensory experience. All of this takes place behind a simple, domestic-looking proscenium that Johnson borrowed from the ancient Roman theater. It is a simple stage front, called a *scaenae frons*, with three arches through which one can see and hear the thunderous downthrust of water. Houstonians love the place, and so do visitors. Author Frank Welch calls it "the building's pièce de résistance"; architecture professors have made it the first stop on a design tour of the city; and locals have their pictures taken here and stage informal weddings.

Inside the lobby of Williams Tower, a sixty-foot-tall classically arched entry of pink granite, visitors are greeted by four giant paintings, framed and installed as murals, by Ettore Caser (1880–1944): *The Four Branches of Engineering*. Since the tower was inspired by the terraced stone skyscrapers of the 1920s and 1930s, these paintings capture some of the excitement of the building. They were originally commissioned for the New York Engineers Club and painted in the 1920s to show all of the field's endeavors. *Civil* outlines a ship looming in the background; *Mining* depicts donkeys on a mountain trail and a train loaded with ore; *Electricity* indicates man's harnessing of natural power; while *Mechanical* shows a skyscraper being magnificently raised.

Inside the lobby of Williams Tower, a sixty-foot-tall classically arched entry of pink granite, visitors are greeted by four giant paintings, framed and installed as murals, by Ettore Caser: *The Four Branches of Engineering*. They were originally commissioned for the New York Engineers Club and painted in the 1920s to show all of the field's endeavors. *Civil* outlines a ship looming in the background; *Mining* depicts donkeys on a mountain trail and a train loaded with ore; *Electricity* indicates man's harnessing of natural power; while *Mechanical* shows a skyscraper being raised.

The Williams Tower Water Wall. A sixty-four-foot-high curved wall of black obsidian sets off the crash of 11,800 gallons of water per minute that finishes on a gently curving ring of steps at the bottom. The cataract comes down the front and the back side of the giant wall. All of this takes place behind a simple, domestic-looking proscenium that Philip Johnson borrowed from the ancient Roman theater. It is a simple stage front, called a *scaenae frons*, with three arches through which one can see and hear the thunderous cascade of water.

In 1984, Johnson played a major role in another very public work of art, this one at 580 California in San Francisco. 580 California is a twenty-three-story, neo-French Gothic tower in pale granite with rows of bay windows and topped by a two-story mansard roof in black reflective glass. On the top of each of the building's twelve supporting columns—three columns on each of the four sides of the structure—are twelve remarkable figures Johnson commissioned from New York sculptor Muriel Castanis (born in 1926), called *Three Models for 580 California*. On the crown of this serious San Francisco financial district building stands a surprising sorority of toga-sporting blithe spirits, waving their scarves along the roofline. They are twelve-foot-tall shells—hooded figures, but ones that have no bodies beneath the windswept clothing.

"Muriel Castanis had to create a wire sculpture on a human scale, drape this material over it, and then send it somewhere else to do it in the size we needed to look proportionally right on top of the building," remembers Hines' Owens. "The glass mansard roof wasn't really a roof—it was occupied floors—so that if you were on that floor, you looked out, or around, or through those sculptures. People in San Francisco started calling them the twelve judges or the twelve apostles or wondered whether they were supposed to be the twelve San Francisco city councillors."

Owens remembers that it was not so easy to have the local authorities sign off on the sculptures. "They have very firm control over architecture in San Francisco," Owens explains. "The San Francisco Redevelopment Agency questioned why this was art. Philip had a lot of pictures of buildings in Versailles and France and ancient Rome, where sculpture was very much a part of the architecture. We had to convince the city of San Francisco that this wasn't frou-frou—that it had real purpose and meaning and context."

Castanis, who is known for her works in cloth, once explained that earlier in her career she discovered that cleaning rags, when soaked in glue, could be used as a sculpting medium. The 580 California figures are made of fabric, epoxy, and fiberglass.

In 1986, Gerald D. Hines Interests commissioned another monumental sculpture, this time for 31 West 52nd Street in New York. The thirty-story, pale granite structure, originally home to E. F. Hutton and now Deutsche Bank, was designed by Kevin Roche John Dinkeloo and Associates. It shares a public plaza with the home to CBS corporate headquarters, known as Black Rock, a block-long space between 52nd and 53rd Streets, across from the Museum of Modern Art. This plaza is home to a monumental work by Jesús Bautista Moroles (born in 1950), *Lapstrake*. The twenty-two-foot-tall, sixty-four-ton work in gray granite is one of the most significant public sculptures in Manhattan. The totemic structure has two thick, rounded columns intersected by a series of rectangular slabs sliding irregularly downward.

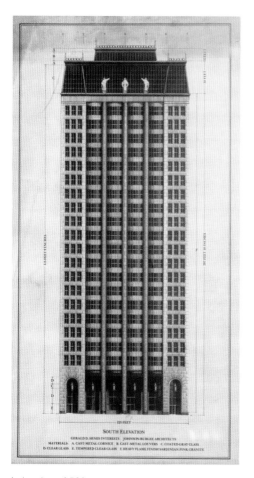

A drawing of 580 California by Johnson and Burgee, above, and the constructed property at right, featuring three of a dozen figures created by New York sculptor Muriel Castanis. Called *Three Models for 580 California*, each twelve-foot-tall sculpture crowns a supporting column. Earlier in her career, Castanis discovered that cleaning rags, when soaked in glue, could be used as a sculpting medium. The 580 California figures are made of fabric, epoxy, and fiberglass.

An art exhibit in the lobby of 31 West 52nd Street in New York, which is open to the public. The thirty-story, pale granite structure, originally home to E. F. Hutton and now Deutsche Bank, shares a public plaza with the CBS corporate headquarters. The block-long space between 52nd and 53rd Streets, across from the Museum of Modern Art, is home to a granite sculpture by Jesús Bautista Moroles called *Lapstrake*.

At left, *Lapstrake*, by
Jesús Bautista Moroles.
The twenty-two-foot-
tall, sixty-four-ton work
in gray granite is one
of the most imposing
public sculptures in
Manhattan. Right,
L.A. Prime Matter, a
thirty-six-foot work
by sculptor Eric Orr,
graces Figueroa
at Wilshire in Los
Angeles. A square
base is topped by two
triangular columns
flowing with water and
a ridge of fire.

Born in Corpus Christi, Texas, Moroles now lives and works in nearby Rockport. From his studio he has conceived some of America's largest sculptures, winning praise for their contemplative, poetic qualities that are especially impressive for work at such an enormous scale. As one critic noted, "The work of Jesús Bautista Moroles continues to astonish because of his capacity to extract new poetry and pose new paradoxes in one of the most adamantine materials on earth: granite, the stone 'born of fire.' The sheer tonnage of the work is belied by Moroles' richly textured, strangely immaterial surfaces sparkling with countless facets of quartz and feldspar. In Manhattan, for example, his gigantic *Lapstrake*, at E. F. Hutton Plaza, unfailingly transfixes office workers and visitors on their way to the Museum of Modern Art."

The following year, 1987, Hines turned to architect Cesar Pelli for the fifty-seven-story Norwest Center (now the Wells Fargo Center) in Minneapolis. The soaring structure, with slabs of buff limestone softened by a series of setbacks, is an homage to Raymond Hood's famous GE Building in Rockefeller Center. Instead of settling on a single work of art for the building, however, the developer decided to import an actual museum.

Along a two-block-long stretch of the ground floor of the Wells Fargo Center, a series of exhibition spaces were built and given over to the Minneapolis Institute of Arts. The twenty-one vitrines hold temporary exhibitions of works from the museum's collections, concentrating on all aspects of modernism. One of the most crowded spaces in downtown Minneapolis, the exhibition space is referred to by locals as the "boulevard d'art."

In 1990, Hines turned to architect Albert C. Martin for the dramatic Figueroa at Wilshire in Los Angeles, and sculptor Eric Orr (1939–1998) for a fittingly dramatic work of art. The fifty-two-story building, in coral granite and bronze glass, is a bold geometric form that culminates in an octagonal glass crown. At its base, California sculptor Eric Orr created a dramatic work, *L.A. Prime Matter*, that rises thirty-six feet above the ground. Inspired by his visit to sites in Egypt and Zaire, Orr created a series of fountains combining air, fire, water, and earth (the series was begun in 1981, with a work at the Los Angeles County Museum of Art). For Figueroa at Wilshire, Orr came up with a square base topped by two triangular columns flowing with water and a ridge of fire.

In 1991, Hines returned to Cincinnati

and the next phase of its development there, Chemed Center at 255 Fifth, a thirty-two-story gray granite tower by Skidmore, Owings & Merrill. "When we did the last project on that block, we went to the American Craft Council and found a lady who did four quilts for us that we hung on the wall," remembers Owens. "They represent the four seasons, in the color of the season, and are changed out four times a year." That lady they found was Ellen Kochansky.

Kochansky has voiced a fascinating philosophy for her career: "The things we throw away are all still with us. If transforming them thoughtfully into images or products that remind us of our history or our wastefulness or our unfinished business, can be a life's work, I'm on it." As the artist, whose quilts are on permanent exhibit at the White House, describes it, "My work is about the content rather than the surface, in both two and three dimensions. I am exploring the humble, somewhat random debris generated by our lives on the planet."

In 1999, Hines worked with Los Angeles architect Frank Gehry to create a spectacular new building in the capital of Germany for DG Bank Berlin. (The building is now known as DZ Bank.) The mixed-used structure is the Berlin headquarters of the German bank and a residential component with thirty-nine apartments.

Recognized as the designer of the famed Guggenheim Museum in Bilbao and the Disney Concert Hall in Los Angeles (which Hines consulted on), Gehry won a design competition held by the bank. The design began with a quiet, classical façade on Pariser Platz, which was obligated to defer to the historic Brandenburg Gate. But the conventional,

five-story structure in front gives way at the rear of the building to an exuberant, organic apartment building that rises ten stories. The secondary façade features curving planes like large waves and brings to mind Barcelona's famed Antoni Gaudi. Pulling the two pieces together is a powerful architectural statement from Gehry, an atrium that is considered one of the largest in Europe. As the *Architectural Review* described the space, "Flats are separated from the offices by an elliptical void enclosed by a swirling, shimmering glass wall suspended from the roof that cascades down to a pool below. Two glazed lifts glide up and down through the void like air bubbles."

It is in this remarkable atrium that Gehry, shifting from architecture to sculpture, created a mysterious piece: a conference hall that appears to float in space. The four-story-high structure resembles an enormous prehistoric horse's head and is clad in stainless steel on the exterior and wood on the interior. As the critic of *Architectural Record* described it, "The object is just a meeting room in the heart of the building, but its power cannot be denied. Is that a snarling snout that confronts us as we approach it? Is that a single, staring eye off to the left or is it a bit of fabric torn by a wind gust? As the visitor moves around the object, a glazed slit becomes visible, like the hinge between jaw and skull. Somehow, a few dozen metal panels have become feral, suggesting a mammalian form frozen as it struggles against the tight confines of its enclosure. This is the Gehry aesthetic in its most psychologically naked form."

In 1997, city planners in Barcelona

decided to reclaim and redevelop their Mediterranean waterfront by replacing an eyesore: a former rail yard, once hidden behind industrial buildings and maintenance sheds. For the $900 million, ten-year, mixed-use project called Diagonal Mar, Hines worked with architects Enric Miralles and partner Benedetta Tagliabue, principals of the Catalan architecture studio EMBT Arquitectes Associats. One of the largest developments in Europe, Diagonal Mar is an eighty-four-acre project containing fifteen residential buildings, three office towers, three hotels, and a retail center with more than a million square feet designed by Robert A. M. Stern. It also contains the thirty-four-acre Parc Diagonal Mar, one of the largest public parks in the city and the first to apply the principles of sustainable development. Awarded a prize from the American Society of Landscape Architects, Parc Diagonal Mar was hailed by the jury

as "the best constructed wetlands I've ever seen. . . . This is a big success."

Parc Diagonal Mar–opened in 2001 and designed by Miralles–includes playgrounds, shaded seating areas, fountains, a waterfall, an outdoor café, viewing mounds, and a large central lake with fountains and sprays along a path that leads to the sea. Viewed from above by residents, the design is also conceived as an abstract tapestry. It is filled with sculptural elements, including staggered walls in the lake to create falls, bold geometric lines of a footbridge over an area of natural grasses, and a series of tubular stainless steel structures, swooping up and down over the edge of the lake to provide visitors with a cooling mist.

Later that year, Hines inaugurated

Parc Diagonal Mar–opened in 2001 and designed by Enric Miralles and Benedetta Tagliabue–includes a large central lake with fountain, above. The park is filled with sculptural elements, opposite, including staggered walls, a bold geometric footbridge over an area of natural grasses, and a series of tubular stainless steel structures that swoop over the edge of the lake.

Architect Frank Gehry's conference hall within DZ Bank in Berlin, Germany. The four-story high structure, its sculptural form resembling an enormous prehistoric horse's head, is clad in stainless steel on the exterior and wood on the interior.

At left, the lobby of
383 Madison Avenue
features a 1950 mosaic
of the New York City
skyline, originally
commissioned for the
nearby Manhattan
Savings Bank. The
mural was painstakingly
restored.

another building in New York, 383 Madison Avenue, and resurrected a fragment of the city's art history. The forty-five-story structure in dark granite, designed by Skidmore, Owings & Merrill, is the corporate headquarters for Bear Stearns. The lobby has been given over to a 1950 mosaic of the New York City skyline, originally commissioned for the nearby Manhattan Savings Bank (a 1923 building that was demolished in 1998). Signed V. Foscato, a family-run mosaic firm from Long Island City, the grimy mural was soaked in a mud and acid bath before being subjected to a painstaking restoration. Broken tiles were replaced using tweezers and epoxy and a new white background, fourteen by eleven feet, was created from hand-cut Italian glass. As James Lang, the senior managing director of Bear Stearns, told the *New York Times* about the finished work: "My jaw dropped after it was cleaned."

The following year, Hines opened Fourth & Madison in Seattle, a forty-story building in pale granite by local architects Zimmer Gunsul Frasca Partnership. The architects of the critically acclaimed tower had another major attention grabber in the works: in the five-story atrium, a forty-by-sixty-foot iridescent glass curtain wall by New York architect and glass artist Jamie Carpenter. This work is a highly technical achievement, with fifty-six five-by-seven-foot panels of clear glass suspended by a high-tension, stainless steel, cable-grid system. The design of the piece allows for slight movement in the facade. As the wall moves and as the outside light changes, vertical

and horizontal prismatic colored and acid-etched glass fins create a remarkable display of shifting color. The architectural critic for the *Seattle Post-Intelligencer* called it "one of the most sophisticated pieces of public art in Seattle."

That same year, Hines returned to San Francisco and kinetic artist George Rickey. The JPMorgan Chase Building, a thirty-one-story steel and glass structure by Cesar Pelli, has a landscaped park with a black granite fountain at its base. Standing in that fountain is Rickey's *Annular Eclipse*, a thirty-foot kinetic sculpture that features a stainless steel shaft with two rings that move gently in the breeze.

Appropriately enough, as the principal of a firm that has been so focused on public art, Gerald Hines has had plenty of art in his life. His wife, Barbara, has been a painter for the past twenty years and very supportive of the firm's commitment to art. In their Robert A. M. Stern–designed house in Houston is a significant interior sculpture by Henry Moore, while their house in Aspen, designed by Charles Moore, has a major sculpture by Joan Miró.

As Hines remembers, "When we went to see Miró in Spain, he said, 'Gerry, do you like women?'"

"I said, 'Yes, Mr. Miró—I like women.'"

"He said, 'Well, I wanna give you one.' And he gave me a sculpture called *Miss Red Legs*. It's about five or six feet tall—it stands in the entrance to our house."

Gerald Hines is certain the firm will continue to invest in public art. He says that two of its largest current European projects, in Paris and Milan, will feature significant works of art. "It has been important to us for a while now," Hines explains. "It's not our philosophy to collect the last dollar out of everything. Our idea has also been to try to give a little bit back, and it seems to work— we tend to get a lot of new business."

Above, the lobby of Fourth & Madison in Seattle features a forty-by-sixty-foot iridescent glass curtain wall by Jamie Carpenter. Fifty-six panels are suspended by a high-tension, stainless steel, cable-grid system. As the wall moves and the outside light changes, vertical and horizontal prismatic colored and acid-etched glass fins create a display of shifting color.

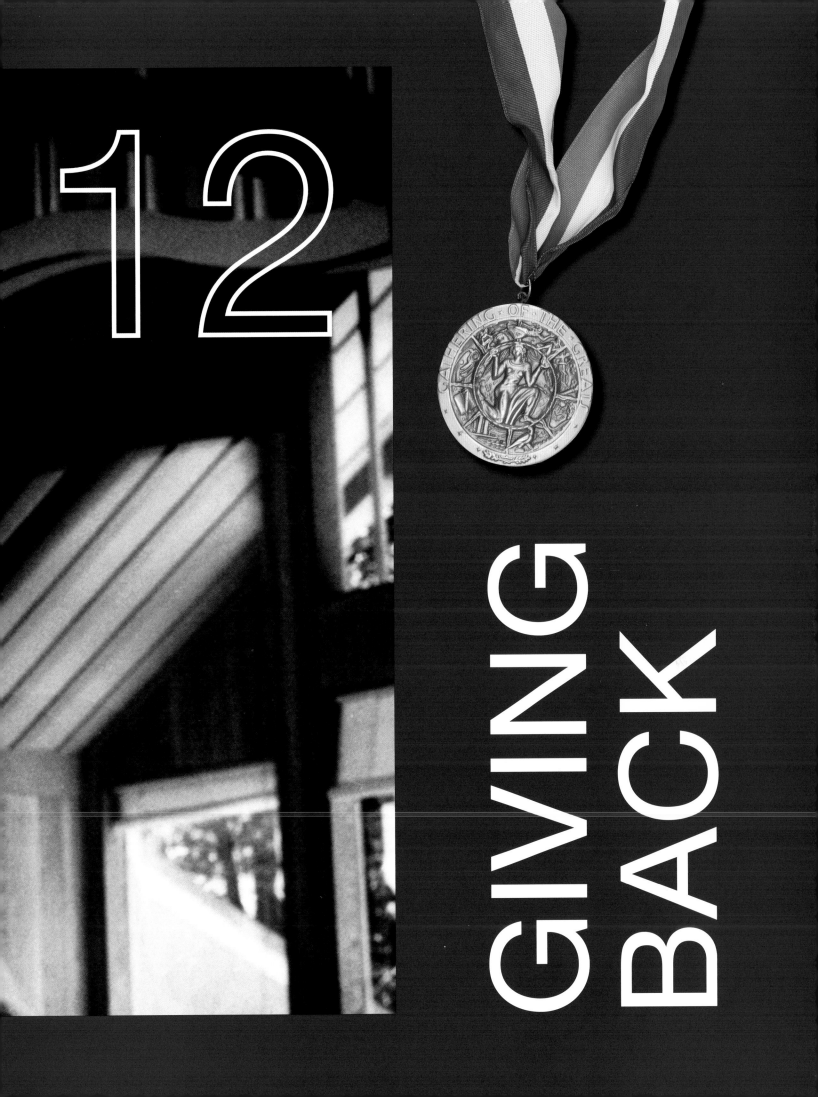

12

GIVING BACK

In 1997, Gerald Hines provided a gift to permanently endow University of Houston's school of architecture. The school was named the Gerald D. Hines College of Architecture. Atop the Philip Johnson–designed building that houses the school is a square, open-roofed Tempietto with a glass floor, which serves as the ceiling of the main building.

Gerald Hines with his mother, Myrtle McConnell Hines. Before she went off to college, Myrtle taught students in a one-room schoolhouse in Nova Scotia. It was she who instilled in Hines the importance of education—the focus of Hines' philanthropic efforts.

People who know Gerald D. Hines remark upon his passion for innovative building, for quality architecture, for the social and physical context of great cities. But the source of energy that has enabled him to accomplish so much in each of those realms is, unquestionably, his passion for people. ▣ Consider that Hines' career as a developer started with a relationship–a serendipitous chat over the backyard fence with his neighbor, whose employer needed a new building. As his company grew, Hines developed a formula for doing business that reflected his deep appreciation for talent: create nimble teams of entrepreneurs; educate and empower them to do their best work; and invite them to share in the rewards of their labors. At the heart of the company's culture is a fundamental faith in the power of people, and it explains why so many Hines executives have dedicated their careers to Gerald Hines and his vision. ▣ "I think that when my dad reflects on his legacy, it's more the organization that has been created and will go on than the buildings themselves," says Jeff Hines, president of the firm. "Yes, he's proud of the buildings and the real estate solutions we've put in place, but he's more proud of the quality of the people we have, and the values and culture we've fostered." ▣ When Gerald Hines built his international operations, for example, he moved slowly and deliberately, because he knew success abroad would hinge on finding the right people in each country. And when he found those people–enthusiastic, intelligent, committed dreamers like himself– he took an interest in them not only as employees, but also as individuals.

As Karl Franz Wambach, head of Hines Germany says, "I was overwhelmed by the personal touch of Gerald D. Hines." That personal touch has forged enduring partnerships with architects, investors, tenants, and employees. So it is not surprising that in his philanthropic activities, Hines has devoted his most significant gifts to fostering young talent in the industry to which he has dedicated his life.

"My father's philanthropy efforts have a directed focus on education as a way to create a better built environment," says Jeff Hines. "He's always been very interested in the creative power of young people, and he gets a great kick out of leaving a tangible impact on the community."

Gerald Hines supported a variety of causes over the years, according to retired executive Louis Sklar, who tracked the Hines family's personal gifts and was responsible for the corporate giving program. "More than thirty years ago, he was one of a very small group of businessmen who founded the Houston-area Urban League," Sklar recalls. "The early gifts tended to be in a broad range of civic endeavors, which really reflected a desire to create a better Houston." They included community organizations ranging from the United Way to the Houston Grand Opera to a plethora of smaller nonprofits that dealt with the care of children, battered women, AIDS, and park conservation.

In the 1990s, Hines turned his focus to significant gifts supporting education, beginning with the University of Houston's College of Architecture. Our institution's humble origins are not unlike Hines' own: the school was founded after World War II on a shoestring budget as part of the College of Engineering, housed in vocational shops. Over the years, the architecture program attracted a diverse faculty that included some of the city's best designers, many of whom maintained active practices and taught in part-time capacities. Similar to the culture at Hines, the emphasis had always been on the quality of the work and the people—in this case, the students.

The college grew and sprouted such distinguished programs as the Honors Studio, which hosted up-and-coming architectural stars as guest instructors; the Texas Studio, which focused on the architecture of the region and grew into a collaboration with Charles Moore's master class at the University of Texas; the Sasakawa International Center for Space Architecture; and a studies center in Saintes, France.

In 1984, the university began construction on a signature building designed by Philip Johnson: four stories of studios arranged around a dramatic skylighted atrium. The square, open-roofed *tempietto* atop the building features a glass floor, which serves as the ceiling of the main building. A deep entrance loggia and extraordinary terrazzo floor are other highlights of the design, which Johnson has said was inspired by the work of eighteenth-century French architect Claude Nicholas Ledoux.

As David Dillon, architecture critic of the *Dallas Morning News* observed in his review of the college for *Architecture* magazine: "Despite the absence of a

grand plan and, until recently, adequate facilities—or maybe because of those factors—UH students consistently turn out excellent work that is rigorous, well made, and ambitious without being cheaply fashionable."

But the college lacked funds to take the programs to the next level. In May 1997, Hines provided a gift to permanently endow the college. "My family and I are very pleased to have the opportunity to participate in the nurturing of the great architects of the next century," Hines said at the time. "We felt that supporting the University of Houston was a way to say thank you to the Houston community at large for its support of our endeavors over the last forty years." In honor of Hines' contribution, the college was renamed the Gerald D. Hines College of Architecture in 1997.

Houston businessman Lee Hogan chaired the University of Houston's $400 million capital campaign in the 1990s, which included expansion of the architecture school. "I think Mr. Hines wanted people to understand how important architecture, design, and aesthetics can be to a community—that motivated the gift," says Hogan. "It clearly was not about notoriety or visibility. Mr. Hines was not enthusiastic about putting his name on the college—he is incredibly generous, but he doesn't seek recognition."

But university officials convinced Hines that his name would help attract additional support. "We convinced him that the work he had done in the community dramatically changed the face of Houston, and that the naming was an appropriate way to continue to encourage that focus on aesthetic excellence in the community," Hogan says. "The gift, plus his name, has had a dramatic impact on the school—the school's

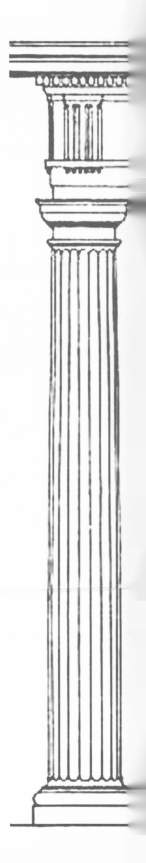

Gerald Hines' major gift to the University of Houston's College of Architecture helped fund a graduate scholarship program, computer imaging equipment, faculty research, and the first industrial design degree program offered in Texas.

recognition has improved significantly in the last decade. The architecture school is now a center of excellence for the university."

The Hines gift came at a very good time for the college, allowing us to reinvigorate our teaching program with visiting critics and an enhanced lecture program at a time when university resources for such extras were running thin. Computer imaging equipment and shop tools to support advanced design work followed. A graduate scholarship program was founded to attract and support excellent graduate students. The college now had the resources to support faculty research and enrichment, including funding travel to present papers and participate in conferences; we have since added an industrial design degree program, the first in Texas.

The Hines Endowment also helped formalize and expand on long-standing ties between the college and the community through the Community Design Center. This center, located in the Hines College, explores innovative solutions to city

building problems, including social spaces; educational, medical, and cultural facilities; urban housing; community development; and transportation. As Hines approached its fiftieth anniversary in 2007, the college was nearing completion of a greatly expanded shop facility and rapid prototyping center named for architect and former professor Burdette Keeland.

The UH College of Architecture flourished in the decade following the Hines gift, and our student population grew at roughly twice the rate of the rest of the university. Although the college utilizes a "blind" review process for program applicants, the diversity of students also increased. In 2006, no ethnic majority existed in the nearly eight-hundred-member student body. More than a thousand applications are reviewed annually for 160 places in our undergraduate programs each year, and test scores for those accepted have risen consistently and substantially. However, admission to the college includes the opportunity to submit a portfolio of work for review, and some applicants who have not tested well continue to be admitted largely on this basis. The college remains focused on talent, ability, and promise as the hallmarks of its successful students.

Beyond the endowment, Gerald Hines sought other ways to nurture individual talent. For example, he facilitated an internship program with Pei Cobb Freed & Partners. He also provided a stipend for students to work with the designers of Diagonal Mar, the Hines company's huge, fifteen-block, mixed-use project on the coast of Barcelona. Oscar Tusquets of the Spanish firm Tusquets, Diaz + Associates was the lead planner for the

McNair Hall, home to
the Jesse H. Jones
Graduate School of
Management at Rice
University, right, where
Gerald Hines provided
the funds for a new
endowed professorship
in real estate
development. Gerald
Hines has served as
a trustee advisor on
the university's board.
The National Building
Museum 2000 Honor
Award, below right,
was given to Gerald
Hines for setting a
standard for design
and innovation.

project, and Spanish landscape architect Enric Miralles was designing a park there. Throughout the development of Diagonal Mar, several students each year had the incomparable experience of living and working in one of the most exciting architectural cities in the world.

Hines' support has encouraged the growth of new relationships. Since the Hines Endowment was initiated, the UH College of Architecture has been able to attract significant additional private support–and our overall operating budget has tripled since 1986. Because the proceeds from the Hines Endowment can be used as needed by the college, the gift remains instrumental across almost every aspect of our operations. The college enjoys a growing reputation among our peer institutions, augmenting our ability to attract the finest faculty members and increasingly stronger applicants to the programs.

Following his generous gift to the UH College of Architecture, Gerald Hines turned his attention to the Jesse H. Jones Graduate School of Management at Rice University, where he provided funds for a new endowed professorship in real estate development. Jones dean William Glick notes that the gift "enabled the school to hire a top real estate scholar who has ignited Rice Master of Business Administration students' interest in real estate. This gift is an investment guided by Gerald Hines' vision of the future of the industry."

The gift helped to catalyze a relationship between the Rice schools of architecture and business, and students who enroll in both programs collaborate on case study development projects. Working with Chris Downing, the first Gerald D. Hines Professor of Real Estate Development, and architecture professor William Cannady, teams consisting of architecture and MBA students worked on a project that combined mid-rise residential units and

Gerald Hines with Senator Pat Moynihan (left) and jury chair Bob Larson (right), receiving the 2002 Urban Land Institute J. C. Nichols Prize for Visionary Urban Development. The prize carries a one-hundred-thousand-dollar honorarium, which Hines declined. ULI used the prize money to establish the ULI Gerald D. Hines Student Urban Design Competition. Opposite, in Milan, Gerald Hines, top, and professor Stefan Behnisch, second from top, talked with Yale students while visiting the future site of the new Museum of Fashion and Design.

retail space with a proposed metro transit center in midtown Houston. The success of the program has prompted consideration of a joint degree program between the two divisions.

Gerald Hines has said that he sees both the Rice University and University of Houston gifts as opportunities for him reinvest in and improve the quality of the future of Houston, where his career as a developer began.

Hines' devotion to design excellence, giving back to the community, and attracting the best and brightest young minds to the industry earned the legendary development pioneer a prestigious honor from the Urban Land Institute (ULI), the highly respected international nonprofit research and education institute devoted to responsible land use. Hines was chosen as the 2002 laureate of the Urban Land Institute J. C. Nichols Prize for Visionaries in Urban Development, an annual prize that recognizes lifelong contributions to the highest land-use standards and extraordinary community building accomplishments. The prize carries a one hundred thousand dollar honorarium, which Hines declined, and which ULI chose to devote to the establishment of the ULI Gerald D. Hines Student Urban Design Competition.

The competition challenges interdisciplinary teams of graduate students from universities all around the United States to offer practical, workable solutions to an urban design and development problem identified at an actual site in a

major urban area. Gerald Hines contributed an additional one hundred thousand dollars to inaugurate the competition, and the following year he endowed the program with three million dollars to fund it in perpetuity. "The purpose of the competition is to raise awareness, particularly among the next generation, of the important role high-quality urban design plays in creating not just beautiful buildings, but living environments," Hines says.

Winning team member Christina Cambruzzi, who was studying urban planning, appreciated the experience the competition provided. "I learned more during the competition than I had during my entire time in the graduate program. The chance to work on an interdisciplinary team was a unique opportunity."

The competition encourages cooperation and teamwork among future real estate developers and the many allied professions such as architecture, landscape architecture, urban planning, historic preservation, engineering, finance, psychology, and law. "Real estate development is a very exciting, imaginative field. It involves many disciplines and interaction with so many parts of our world—finance, politics, science, psychology—it affects the lives of so many people," Hines says. "Through this competition, students get hands-on, real world experience in urban design, and the possibility of their ideas being turned into a lasting community improvement."

The winning team is awarded fifty thousand dollars, and finalists split thirty thousand dollars. Since the program's creation, the students have tackled assignments in Washington, D.C.,

Pittsburgh, Salt Lake City, and St. Louis. "Gerry's desire to create an interdisciplinary urban design competition was brilliant," says ULI president Richard M. Rosan. "Because of this competition, students at several universities have formed real estate clubs that cross disciplines, bringing designers together with business students. Time and time again, students tell us that although the competition is one of the hardest things they've ever done, particularly with regard to working in cross-disciplinary teams, it's also one of their most rewarding learning experiences. It brings together so much of what the Urban Land Institute stands for and teaches about real estate development being a multidisciplinary process."

Having influenced the education of architects through his philanthropy, Gerald Hines took part in a program that would allow him to be more directly involved with studio teaching. In 2005 Hines served as the inaugural fellow for the Edward P. Bass Distinguished Visiting Architecture Fellowship at the Yale School of Architecture. The program brings property developers together with senior design students to review an active development project in the fellow's firm. The project that Hines posed to the students was Milan's Garibaldi Repubblica, a site in the city center being master-planned by Pelli Clarke Pelli.

Along with students and the visiting professor with whom he was teamed, Stefan Behnisch, Hines visited the site and returned to Yale to collaborate with the students on a design for the Museum of Fashion and Design, which the developer hoped would serve as a cultural centerpiece to the site. "We thought it would be more interesting for a studio to design the fashion museum rather than the office component," says

Hines, "so the students got a chance to take a first crack at this."

The legacy of Gerald Hines is illustrated by his desire to lead by example—making contributions to urban areas that withstand the test of time, and setting a course of excellence for future generations of community builders. "Gerry is a visionary in every sense of the word," says Rosan. "Through his personal integrity, his uncompromising commitment to high quality, his pursuit of environmental sustainability, and his desire to give back to his profession and to communities in general, Gerry has created a success formula few can emulate. He has shown, many times over, that design and quality do matter, and our built environment is all the better for it."

Over the last fifty years, Gerald Hines has been driven by a passion for excellence. He is most inspired by the exchange of ideas—as intrigued by novel architecture as he is by pragmatic engineering innovations that lower costs or improve efficiency. Hines has never lost sight of the fact that his buildings have soared and skylines have been transformed through the ingenuity and collaboration of individuals.

His most lasting legacy is not in the skyline, but in the people.

"You always learn something from the students; they are great young minds to interact with," Hines says of his work at Yale. "You learn something with every encounter—and that is what life is about."

ABOUT THE
CONTRIBUTORS

David Childs is consulting design partner at Skidmore, Owings & Merrill/ New York. He has completed a wide range of projects in locations around the globe. A graduate of Yale College and the Yale School of Art and Architecture, Childs joined the Washington, D.C., office of Skidmore, Owings & Merrill in 1971. From 1975 to 1981, he served as chairman of the National Capital Planning Commission. In 2002, he received a presidential appointment to the Commission of Fine Arts in Washington, where he served as chairman. His current civic involvements include membership on the boards of the Museum of Modern Art and the Municipal Art Society, and the chairmanship of the Academy in Rome. He is a Fellow of the American Institute of Architects.

Paul Goldberger is the architecture critic for *The New Yorker*, which he joined in 1997 after a twenty-five-year career at the *New York Times*, where his writing won the Pulitzer Prize. He also holds the Joseph Urban Chair in Design and Architecture at Parsons The New School in New York. He is the author of several prominent books on architecture and design, and lectures extensively around the world on architecture, design, and historic preservation. In addition to his work at The New School, where he has also served as dean, he has taught at Yale and Berkeley. Goldberger's writing has garnered the President's Medal of the Municipal Art Society of New York, the medal of the American Institute of Architects, the Roger Starr Journalism Award from the Citizens Housing and Planning Council, and the New York City Landmarks Preservation Commission's Preservation Achievement Award from former mayor Rudolph Giuliani.

Lisa Gray serves as the arts editor at the *Houston Chronicle*, and is a freelance book editor and writer whose pieces have appeared in numerous magazines. She has been a staff writer and columnist for the *Houston Press* and managing editor at *Cite: The Architectural and Design Review of Houston*, a quarterly publication for the Design Alliance at Rice University. Gray was the recipient of the 1997 Best Feature Story award from the Houston Press Club. In 2001, she was a finalist for the James Beard Foundation Award for Feature Writing Without Recipes.

Ann Holmes, prize-winning writer and fine arts editor of the *Houston Chronicle* for sixty years, retired from the newspaper as critic-at-large in 2002. Holmes is the author of three books on art and architecture and is currently working on a book about the dynamics of the changing arts scene that is to be published by Texas A&M University Press. She has won the Texas Society of Architects prize in architectural writing four times, in 1972, 1974, 1977, and 1980.

Hilary Lewis is the coauthor of several books on architecture and urbanism, including a collaborative work that features interviews with esteemed architect and Hines partner Philip Johnson and *THINK New York: A Ground Zero Diary*. An expert on urban planning, architecture, and real estate development, Lewis has taught at Harvard and the Massachusetts Institute of Technology. She has been a featured author at the Texas Book Festival and is a recipient of the American Institute of Architects International Book Award. Renowned for her work on Johnson, she serves as an advisor to the National Trust for Historic Preservation, which owns the Glass House, Johnson's former home.

Joe Mashburn is the dean of the Gerald D. Hines College of Architecture at the University of Houston in Texas. He is the recipient of the Association of Collegiate Schools of Architecture Design Award, the Virginia Society AIA Award for Excellence in Architecture, the Texas Society of Architects Honor Award for Design Excellence, and the Committee of Heads of Australian Schools of Architecture Design Award. Mashburn has served as an assistant professor and graduate design coordinator at Texas A&M University and is a member of the school's Architecture Hall of Fame. Mashburn has also served as head of the architecture department at Curtin University of Technology in Perth, Australia, and has taught at the School of Architecture and Fine Arts at the University of Western Australia and Virginia Tech in the United States.

William McDonough is a world-renowned architect and the founding principal of two sustainable design firms, William McDonough + Partners Architecture and Community Design and McDonough Braungart Design Chemistry. From 1994 to 1999 he served as the dean of the School of Architecture at the University of Virginia, and in the final year of his tenure *Time* magazine named him a Hero for the Planet. McDonough has also been honored with several of the nation's most prestigious awards, including the Presidential Award for Sustainable Development in 1996, the Presidential Green Chemistry Challenge Award in 2003, and the Smithsonian Institution's Cooper Hewitt Design Museum's National Design Award in 2004. With the German chemist Michael Braungart, he is the author of *The Hannover Principles: Design for Sustainability*, and the influential design manifesto *Cradle to Cradle: Remaking the Way We Make Things*.

William Middleton is an accomplished publisher, writer, and editor. He has served as the Paris bureau chief for Fairchild Publications, overseeing the production of *W* and *Women's Wear Daily*. His written work has appeared in the pages of numerous high-fashion periodicals, including *Vogue*, *Vogue Hommes International*, *Vogue Italia*, and *Harper's Bazaar*. He has also authored biographical essays and profiles on celebrities and figures in pop culture for *Vibe*, *Esquire*, and *Out* magazines, as well as pieces for the *International Herald Tribune* and the *New York Times*. He resides in Houston, where he is writing a biography of prominent Houstonians John and Dominique de Menil.

Ron Nyren has written numerous articles for periodicals such as *Interior Design*, *Metropolis*, *Urban Land*, *Urban Land Asia*, *Dialogue*, and *AEC* magazine, as well as the online journals *ArchitectureWeek*, *ArchNewsNow*, and *LINE*. As a writer and editor of communications materials for the design and development industries, Nyren has also helped produce proposals, monographs, project descriptions, award submittals, Web text, and press releases. He lives and works in the San Francisco Bay Area.

William J. Poorvu, is the author of numerous books and articles on real estate, including *The Real Estate Game*. He serves as the Class of 1961 Adjunct Professor in Entrepreneurship Emeritus at Harvard Business School, where he taught the course in real estate for many decades. He has been an independent director of several public REITs as well as of a large mutual fund group. He has also been a managing partner and consultant for several real estate companies as well as other organizations in the private and public spheres.

Laura Rowley is a columnist for Yahoo!Finance and *Self* magazine and the author of three books on business and personal finance. She is a former producer/reporter for CNN Business News, and her freelance work has been featured in the *New York Times*, *Parents*, *Babytalk*, and other publications. Rowley also served as the editor-in-chief of *Multi Housing News*, a trade magazine for builders and developers.

Mark Seal has collaborated on multiple best-selling nonfiction books. A contributing editor to *Vanity Fair*, he began his career as a reporter for Texas newspapers, including the *Houston Chronicle* and the *Dallas Morning News*. Becoming a freelance writer in 1984, he has written for periodicals including *Esquire*, *Allure*, *Town & Country*, *Time*, *Texas Monthly*, *Golf Digest*, *Rolling Stone*, *Conde Nast Traveler*, and the *New York Times*. Since 1990 he has written a bi-weekly column for *American Way*, the magazine of American Airlines, in which celebrities discuss their favorite cities. He is the recipient of the 2000 Western Publishers Association Award for Best Column and the 1999 Clarion Award by National Women in Broadcasting.

Robert A. M. Stern serves as the dean of the Yale School of Architecture and is also the founding and senior partner of Robert A. M. Stern Architects in New York City. A teacher, writer, and practicing architect, he received the AIA New York Chapter's Medal of Honor in 1984 and its President's Award in 2001. Stern has coauthored several books, including *New York 1930: Architecture and Urbanism Between the Two World Wars*, which was nominated for a National Book Award. Among his design accomplishments are the Ohrstrom Library at the St. Paul's School in Concord, New Hampshire; the Norman Rockwell Museum in Stockbridge, Massachusetts; and the Feature Animation Building in Burbank, California.